Special Praise for I͟r͟r͟e͟l͟a͟t͟i͟o͟n͟s͟h͟i͟p

"*Irrelationship* crosses the frontier of self-help into a new area the authors call 'self-other help.' The DREAM Sequence used for recovery from irrelationship is designed for couples to work *together* and help them reconnect with the wonderful chemistry and emotional connections that initially drew them to one another."

Diana Kirschner, PhD, best-selling author of *Love in 90 Days*

"A well-written, informative, and entertaining volume that tells us much about ourselves in our loving and not-so-loving relationships with others. A book to read for those brave enough to look inside themselves for understanding."

Tom Gullotta, editor of *Family Influences on Childhood Behavior and Development*, author, and CEO of the Child and Family Agency

"Written for individuals and couples who find their relationships to be unsatisfying, Borg, Brenner, and Berry do a masterful job of combining psychoanalytic theory with cutting edge research from neurobiology, all in completely non-jargon, understandable language. The authors identify factors that contribute to a sense of 'stuckness' in relationships and use clinical vignettes to illustrate the difficulties and demonstrate ways to ameliorate the problems. Helpful for clinicians as well as laypeople."

Susan Kolod, PhD, Training and Supervising Analyst, William Alanson White Institute, and editor of *Psychology Today's* "Contemporary Psychoanalysis in Action"

"Irrelationship is a new label for the old idea of dysfunctional relationships in dating, marital, or partnering couples. With many case studies, the authors describe forms of dysfunction stemming from a psychoanalytic perspective of carrying forward into adulthood the dysfunctional patterns that were formed unconsciously in childhood.

The road to recovery is stated in user-friendly, self-help terms that empower each person in the relationship to make changes and develop healthier ways of thinking and behaving through a mutuality of experience that permits the expression of love in all its wonderful, vital, unpredictable, and even downside forms, as the way to find continued growth and collaboration for both members of the couple."

Martin Bloom, PhD, Professor Emeritus,
University of Connecticut, and editor of *Encyclopedia of Primary Prevention and Health Promotion*

"*Irrelationship* is an invaluable user's guide to the care and maintenance of adult relationships. It shines a light on challenges we often choose to ignore—the adoption of roles that limit us, the replaying of damaging patterns formed by our earliest experiences—and offers insightful and concrete advice on how to do the work necessary to build stronger and happier partnerships."

Carolyn Parkhurst, author of *The Dogs of Babel* and *The Nobodies Album*

IRRELATIONSHIP

How We Use
DYSFUNCTIONAL RELATIONSHIPS
to Hide from Intimacy

IRELATIONSHIP

How We Use
DYSFUNCTIONAL RELATIONSHIPS
to Hide from Intimacy

Mark B. Borg, Jr., PhD., Grant H. Brenner, MD, and
Daniel Berry, RN, MHA

CENTRAL RECOVERY PRESS

LAS VEGAS

Central Recovery Press (CRP) is committed to publishing exceptional materials addressing addiction treatment, recovery, and behavioral healthcare topics, including original and quality books, audio/visual communications, and web-based new media. Through a diverse selection of titles, we seek to contribute a broad range of unique resources for professionals, recovering individuals and their families, and the general public.

For more information, visit www.centralrecoverypress.com.

Publisher: Central Recovery Press
3321 N. Buffalo Drive
Las Vegas, NV 89129

20 19 18 17 16 15   1 2 3 4 5

ISBN: 978-1-942094-00-5 (paper)
       978-1-942094-01-2 (e-book)

Photos of Mark B. Borg, Jr., Grant Brenner, and Daniel Berry by Eric Jiaju Lee.

Publisher's Note: This book contains general information about relationships, recovery, and related matters. The information is not medical advice and should not be treated as such. Central Recovery Press makes no representations or warranties in relation to the information in this book. If you have specific questions about any medical matter discussed in this book, you should consult your doctor or other professional healthcare provider. This book is not an alternative to medical advice from your doctor or other professional healthcare provider.

Our books represent the experiences and opinions of their authors only. Every effort has been made to ensure that events, institutions, and statistics presented in our books as facts are accurate and up-to-date. To protect their privacy, the names of some of the people, places, and institutions in this book have been changed.

Cover design and interior design and layout by Deb Tremper, Six Penny Graphics

To those beloved with whom I *just take a walk*
every day—Haruna, Kata, and Uta.

Mark

For Marina, Quinn, and Reyd, who keep me on my toes.

Grant

To the King of my heart—you know who you are.

Danny

Table of Contents

Acknowledgments

Our agent, Gareth Esersky, gets first mention. She saw what this book was—almost before we did—and guided us through the surprisingly complicated process of bringing our relatively simple and straightforward project to print and to the public eye. She never wavered in her encouragement and her belief in the work's value.

Gareth turned us on to Ilene Segalove. Ilene, an artist and writer of considerable note, made no secret of how taken she was with our project. From her first reading, she knew how to shape the text to make it readable and usable. Her generosity of heart and mind warmed and encouraged us at points when warm and encouraged wasn't necessarily how we were feeling. Ilene also gave us insight into subtleties of the book's revolutionary "self-other help" model, which nudged the manuscript in a direction we had not anticipated and much to its improvement.

Working with Central Recovery Press has been a pleasure, and not just for the spirit of the individuals who coached, taught, and mentored us—Valerie Killeen, Janet Ottenweller, and Nancy Schenck—but also for the shared values vital to having this project realized without compromise of ideas and ideals.

Eve Golden's expertise as a clinician as well as a writer and editor has been essential to our unpacking the psychoanalytic underpinnings of irrelationship. Her relationship with Mark Borg goes back many years, during which she has generously provided not only her talent but also her insightful, affectionate guidance through earlier projects that have culminated in this one.

Sue Kolod of *Psychology Today's* blog, "Contemporary Psychoanalysis in Action," saw to it that irrelationship got its first hearing in cyberspace, and *Psychology Today* editors Kaja Perina and Jessica Mooney gave us our own blogspace for *Irrelationship,* providing a much needed opportunity to test the waters with our ideas. Our friend and mentor Hara Estroff Marano, Editor-at-Large at *Psychology Today,* is a constant source of support and inspiration! We can't express our thanks enough.

From Mark Borg

My first remembrance of love and gratitude goes to my grandmother, Charlotte Rolland, who, without fail, supported me through the most difficult periods of my life. Without her unconditional love, the outcome of some very difficult times would have been dramatically different from what has turned out. I remember her with love and thankfulness every day.

My mother and stepfather, Charlotte and Jon Rysanek, have been loving and supportive all my life—sometimes when I didn't make it easy for them. My father, Mark, and his generous-hearted wife, Bonnie, and my in-laws, Osamu and Yoko Miyamoto, have always been ready and willing to offer support and love to me and to my beautiful wife and daughters.

Huge thanks to Erik and Sandy Borg—who, in a crucial moment, helped me find my way onto the road upon which I continue to trudge.

Much love to my earliest soul mates in All Nite Rave—that's you, Jim DeLozier and your awesome parents Terry and Joan.

Massive gratitude to those whose professional support lives in me every day: Joerg Bose, Maggie Decker, Roger Mills, Joseph Solomita, Sandra Buechler, and Brian Sweeney.

And, wave upon wave of gratitude and love for those who continue to sustain my soul: Chris Borg, Mike Dalla, John (Purple) Turi, Kristy (La Sirena) Matthews, Bill Zunkel, Chris Mertz, Jeanne Henry, Byron Abel,

Greg Hex, Jason Kaja, Tim Barnes, David Kopstein, Seal Beach Surf Crew (wearin' "Dog Shoes"), 12th Street, and Ronda Hampton. Wouldn't have made it without y'all!

It should go without saying—but I'm not going to allow it to—that my utmost gratitude goes to my partners, friends, and coauthors, Grant and Danny, without whom this project could never have gotten from Zero to One.

Foreword

The basic premise of this book—that many people looking for love, or those who believe they have already found it, unwittingly create dysfunctional relationships as a way of keeping true intimacy at arm's length—reflects a fact that marriage and family therapists see day after day in their offices and that many "civilians" just soldier through day after disappointing day. Rarely, however, does anyone ever articulate the phenomenon with such simplicity and clarity or label it so tellingly—irrelationship. So this book arrives as a needed blast of fresh air, to advance everyone's understanding of how people can yearn for love, even make sacrifices for it, and still feel distant from a partner and deeply unsatisfied.

People construct irrelationships because intimacy can be tough work. It's for grown-ups, definitely not for wimps. It is liberating, once attained, but getting there can be anxiety provoking. To achieve intimacy, to be open to it, takes courage. We have to be able to drop our defenses, often deeply ingrained, and stand naked to ourselves, exposing the primal fear that we are flawed and unlovable. Small wonder we often have strong psychological defenses against it. Yet there is no elixir as great as deeply connecting with another human being.

Just who is candidate for an irrelationship? There's no way to judge by external markers. As the authors explain, much depends on the way each of us was exposed to love when young; the "rules" we inferred or explicitly learned long before we knew we were absorbing them, to say nothing of how they might shape our lives; and our tolerance for discomfort. Couples can be locked into patterns of mutual deception for years, living a so-called counterfeit connection. While our early understandings and adaptations may have served us very well in the situations in which we were raised, they can keep us from getting what, as adults in new circumstances, we most want. It is an axiom of psychology that the greatest obstacle in our way is often…ourselves.

The authors of this book bring together a great deal of information from many areas of psychology and psychiatry, along with years of practical experience, to help people understand how they get into irrelationships, how such relationships can take on a life of their own, and how it is possible to break free and create a real relationship. You, reader, are in good hands.

Hara Estroff Marano
Editor at Large, *Psychology Today*

Introduction

All the Wrong Reasons

People love for different reasons, some of which work better than others. We all have ideas about what love and loving are, but where do those ideas come from, and how do they lead or mislead us in choosing a partner? If we ask ourselves what we look for in a mate, we probably answer that we seek passion, empathy, novelty, and security. It sounds sensible and mature and might even be true. But over time, deep down and hidden from ourselves, many of us internalize concepts about love, learned from early childhood, that actually work against finding and cultivating satisfying relationships. Like termites infesting a beautiful old home, these ideas may actually have infiltrated our ways of loving so thoroughly that without realizing it, they undermine our desire for closeness and our ability to accept intimacy. This leads to relationships that can repeatedly leave us feeling disappointed, frustrated, and strangely alienated from those to whom we believe we are closest. Despite our conscious determination that "this time it's going to be different," we end up loving, once again, for all the wrong reasons.

Relationship, rather than being a forum for vulnerability, spontaneity, and freedom can, ironically, be used as a psychological defense. The term used to describe this deceptive trap is *irrelationship*. Irrelationship unconsciously creates false connections to keep others from getting too close, protecting us from the emotional messiness as well as the rewards of intimacy that are part of real relationships. In irrelationship, give and take is perceived as threatening and connections with others are unsatisfying. Expectations and demands are never met because neither party in irrelationship is sufficiently openhearted to be able to receive or reveal their true needs or desires. In this stifling setup, mutually healthy and loving relationships cannot develop.

In their years of clinical practice, the authors have repeatedly encountered patients with histories of tightly controlled, superficial relationships driven by anxiety and fear dating from early childhood. This anxiety was spawned by a childhood environment in which the child's basic need for security was not adequately addressed by caregivers—usually the parents—who themselves were suffering from long-term, negative emotional states. These negative emotional states resulted in neglect of the child's needs, prompting the child to unconsciously attempt to stabilize the care environment, usually by trying to make the caregiver feel better, so that the child felt more secure. Therefore, irrelationship is a relational maladaptation. It's not an illness, syndrome, or pathology but rather a dynamic that the child and parent construct together to circumvent the vulnerability associated with intimacy.

The recovery tools found in this book illuminate the origins and pattern of irrelationship and provide a technique for disempowering it and transforming the individual's isolation into the ability to form genuine, open, and intimate relationships. In addition, the book provides insight into physiological mechanisms in the brain related to the irrelationship pattern and how those patterns can be altered, creating space and grounding for healthy patterns of relating.

The Birth of Irrelationship

Our first encounters with the world (that is to say, with our parents or caregivers), along with inborn predispositions such as genetic and epigenetic factors,[1] mold our early expectations of relationship. Early childhood survival mechanisms and traumas ultimately shape how we approach every relationship thereafter. These interactions actually become hardwired into how our brain processes information about connecting with other people. Imaging of attachment-related differences in a child's brain, if done, would likely reveal distinct patterns of activity as a result of different dynamics in the parent-child connection. A child whose mother wants constant attention is likely to come to a different understanding of love than a child whose mother is comfortable being on the sidelines. A child whose every impulse and whim are catered to will be wired to understand love differently than the child who learned to do all of the catering and caregiving on his or her own. Some parents want to control everything their children do, while others leave their children alone so much that they have to make some types of decisions at an inappropriately young age. Whatever the case, children always respond to their parents' patterns of relating. They exercise little or no conscious choice in this adaptation because they are totally dependent on their parents for survival. They simply do what they need to do to feel safe.

We quickly learn our parents' relational rules; they are so much a part of our environment that unless the rules are called to our attention, we seldom become aware of them. Some rules—like never asking for anything or always having to feel grateful—may leave us feeling isolated or empty, but we follow them for the sake of emotional safety and to ensure the fulfillment of basic needs. Unwittingly, we shape ourselves to the roles parents assign us and continue acting in these roles in future adult relationships. We call these patterns our *song-and-dance routines.* Very early in life, we silently agreed to take care of our parents by following their rules so they would take care of us. If our caregiver was depressed, anxious, or unhappy we did what we could to make him or her feel better. This enmeshed caretaking pattern (i.e., irrelationship) quietly became the defining dynamic of how we related to others, ultimately preventing true connection and intimacy.

A Little Attachment Theory Goes a Long Way

While high-functioning people may appear emotionally sturdy and secure with themselves and others, in reality, the effects of irrelationship have so locked down their emotions that all they have achieved is a sustained effort to conceal an insecure *attachment style,* a term used by psychoanalysts and researchers to describe categorical patterns of how people relate in intimate settings. Attachment theory correlates adult-relatedness with developmental experiences with primary caregivers, describing various attachment styles.[2] The façade created by people affected by irrelationship often proves to be an overcompensation intended to deflect attention—theirs and others'—from anxiety they've suffered all their lives as a result of ineffective parental caregiving. As one might expect, the façades created by irrelationship are usually exposed for what they are and lead to concrete problems that necessitate more effectively addressing the underlying anxiety.

According to attachment theory, we learn how to relate to the world based on the contact we had with our closest caregivers—usually our parents—when we were very small. We bring how we related with them into future relationships so that our manner of relating becomes a product of how our caregivers related with us, i.e., their own attachment style, which developed when *they* were young in relation to *their* caregivers. The greater the demand for intimacy in adult relationships, the more crucial the operation of our attachment style becomes, depending on how intensely and in what ways our early attachments resonate with adult situations.

Attachment styles are generally classified as either secure or insecure (i.e., avoidant or anxious), depending on the quality of caregiving that occurred between child and caregiver; the innate factors with which the child is born; and the fit between the child and the caregiver's attachment styles.[3] People with a secure attachment style develop an inner base early in life that allows them to remain essentially grounded during emotional disruptions or even during severe life crises. They're able to allow themselves to feel emotions and upsets without becoming deeply disturbed and resume equilibrium relatively quickly.

In contrast, the person with insecure attachment style will often find the normal ups and downs of life so anxiety provoking that he or she can manage them only by either dismissing or avoiding them. People with insecure attachment style fall into a few subtypes, including those who avoid or dismiss connection, those who become anxious and preoccupied about connection, and those who have a disorganized mixture of attachment styles.

We can easily see how attachments can snowball rapidly. For example, if a person with an avoidant way of dealing with intimacy gets involved with someone who is anxious and preoccupied, the avoidant person will retreat from the other's advances, evoking a worried pursuit from the anxious person. This makes the avoidant person withdraw even more, setting in motion a cycle that continues until a dramatic resolution—usually unpleasant— occurs. Similarly, a deadening of relationship can develop if two avoidant people meet but leave long-standing dissatisfactions unresolved for extended intervals. In such situations, disappointment and resentment give way to chronic deprivation and suppressed contempt. If communication fails to improve, deep feelings of sadness and grief are added to the mix.

Since one can't necessarily pick and choose the parts of the emotional spectrum to be kept at a distance, the blocking of distressing emotions frequently results in an inability to tolerate *any* type of spontaneous emotional experience, positive or negative. This includes the ability to experience empathy, live compassionately, and fall in love.

Is our experience with early caregivers the last word? Are people living in irrelationship doomed to a life of keeping others at a safe distance and never sharing an intimate relationship?

That's not what attachment theory and the authors' clinical practice seem to indicate. An earned secure attachment is entirely attainable if we're willing to look at our history and do the work of clearing away our confusion about others and ourselves, which allows us to learn how to think more deeply about our emotions and others' feelings and needs. Handling so many moving parts at once is difficult at first and can be an anxiety-triggering deterrent, making irrelationship seem like a more attractive option. But people who make the ongoing choice to address relationship difficulties *do* make progress that they find gratifying on multiple levels.

Our Song-and-Dance Routines

Why is irrelationship so difficult to identify, let alone repair? Why can't being kinder, more generous, or more forgiving eliminate the distress? The answer is that irrelationship reinforces childhood patterns, our original song-and-dance routines, in which we innocently tried to defuse perceived crises by making our caregiver feel better by being good—showing appreciation, being funny or entertaining, showing how smart we were, being as helpful as we could, or simply vanishing from our caregiver's sightline—in short, by applying whatever behavior we could to the crisis to make our caregiver feel better and ourselves feel safer. And it seemed to work; it resulted in a greater sense of peace, or at least less anxiety, allowing us to feel more secure.

Performing jokes for the caregiver may have made things feel lighter, but that isn't the whole story: the child's performance behavior released brain chemicals that gave the child profound feelings of safety and security. After habitual repetition, the song-and-dance routine became the child's signature pattern of relating to others, both behaviorally and on the level of biological brain activity, which is carried into adulthood. Any challenge to this pattern would alarm the child because a change risks short-circuiting the feeling of safety the child worked so hard to create, leading back to the fear and anxiety he or she sought to escape.

A Little Brain Science Also Goes a Long Way

Our ways of relating are more than habits of thinking. Experiences with our first caregivers literally become translated into brain activity that molds the brain's physical structure, and intertwined patterns of network activity reveal themselves in our bodies' physiologic functions and in our behavior. A child will figure out that behaving in a particular way will lead to feeling better. The physical reality underlying this "feel better" behavior the child has learned to deploy triggers recurring patterns of chemical reactions in the brain that are, in fact, the physiologic basis of feeling better. When negative consequences have impressed upon the child the cost of infractions against the rules, the child feels worse, deliberately shaping his or her behavior to agree with parents' expectations. To address the ongoing need for security, the child will enact these roles in virtually all relationships, so that behaving that certain way becomes addictive. An individual can live a lifetime unconscious of how invested he or she has become in these ways of behaving.

Of course unsatisfying adult relationships are the key to recognizing something isn't right. Identifying that one is in irrelationship then becomes the ticket out. In would-be intimate relationships, two people with long-standing anxiety and complementary needs for security will jointly meld into irrelationship and will create a mutual song-and-dance routine. Their routine becomes a technique for managing their insecurity while at the same time taking the place of intimacy. The song-and-dance routine is a ruse that both parties have tacitly agreed to maintain in order to prevent distress.

The Key Players: The Performer and the Audience

There are two key players or roles in the song-and-dance routine that seem to promise connection but actually create a false sense of partnership or intimacy. One is the *Performer,* the overt, apparent caretaker. This person tries to be of service but is often motivated by a need to fix someone out of unconscious reasons. The other is the *Audience,* the individual who subtly takes care of the Performer by needing to be taken care of and craves to be cured or saved but ultimately doesn't want to be fixed at all. The results of this odd partnering is a form of mutual deception. The so-called connection is a form of mutual deception and sadly eliminates any possibility of honest communication or human relatedness. The results are usually that both Performer and Audience feel isolated, devalued, misunderstood, and angry.

The following is a story that spotlights one of the infinite versions of the irrelationship trap. Note that John plays the Performer, and Greta is the Audience.

John and Greta's Irrelationship Storyline

Greta was almost absurdly careful to tell her husband John how much credit he deserved for the trouble he took to make their lives enjoyable. She would gush with pride to John and their friends about his amazing creativity in planning outings. She would go on and on about how carefully he put together guest lists, confirmed reservations, and made sure no detail was overlooked. However, Greta made the mistake of offering to help John with planning their next vacation. John immediately exploded with anger and then caved into hurt and disappointment. He even accused Greta of not appreciating or loving him anymore. In a flash, John revealed a side of himself that Greta had never encountered.

Greta immediately and apologetically took back her suggestion, reassuring John of how much she appreciated everything he did. Greta had gotten a taste of what the consequences would be if she didn't stick with their tightly scripted song-and-dance routine. Although John's burst of anger left Greta feeling frightened and unhappy, she hurriedly retreated back into the carefully, yet unconsciously, constructed status quo of being the Audience, assuring John, the Performer, that nothing had changed. She hoped all of the anxiety would disappear and things would work again.

When sensing danger, the Performer becomes so depressed, anxious, or angry that the Audience fears he or she won't be taken care of, prompting the Audience to fall back into the tried and true song-and-dance routine, hoping to bring the Performer back to the reliable script of irrelationship. Greta's brief attempt to flip their roles provoked such an agitated response from John that she quickly retreated to her Audience role to restore calm. However, the experience left her feeling uneasy, isolated, and depressed. Nevertheless, she did what was necessary to allow John to feel secure again. The brain chemistry that allowed Greta and John to feel secure with one another, although temporarily disturbed, was restored.

John's reaction and the unease Greta felt afterward are clues to the fragility and costliness of the security binding them. This brief disturbance also illustrates the fragility of a relationship that requires an imitation of love that cannot accommodate spontaneity or fluidity. The willingness to accept this type of tenuous agreement mirrors the delicacy of the early childhood bargain John and Greta made with their parents to manage the uncertainty of the environment into which they were born. The tragic outcome of this pattern is that we accept a false kind of love—love that has no flow, no reciprocity, and no room for empathy or compassion. Equally unsettling, we learn that being taken care of is shaky and unreliable and even expect what we call loving relationships to be a series of crises.

People compelled to seek this kind of delicate relationship have an uncanny ability to find their complementary counterpart. When a prospect is identified, hopeful conversations follow as they assess each other's commitment to a carefully defined but static irrelationship role. Ironically, their excitement builds if each person starts to feel that the other can be depended upon to avoid the cardinal sin of looking for mutuality, spontaneity, intimacy, and emotional investment.

So when we seek romantic relationships as adults, our childhood survival routines can cause serious trouble. As Greta learned in her transaction with John, one party is expected to take what the other gives; one is to be the leader while the other accepts the role of follower. One performs and the other must applaud. One saves and the other allows herself to be saved.[4] Love, mutual and intimate, cannot grow under these conditions.

But, what happens if either partner begins to sense a need for something different? What if one individual starts to crave intimacy and reciprocity? Unfortunately, the carefully constructed roles defined by irrelationship don't permit flexible responses. Until the individual (or couple) can grasp how his or her relationship choices are shaped by childhood experience, he or she will remain stuck in a pattern that doesn't support any possibility of trust or genuine love.

The Way Out

Most of us crave authentic, fulfilling relationships free of gratuitous tumult and pain. But to build these relationships requires more than desire; we need a map to help us understand the processes, experiences, and techniques that can free us from the way we've always done things and guide us toward recovery and transformative change. This book presents a clear and engaging examination, diagnosis, and prescription for recovery called the DREAM Sequence. Users of the DREAM Sequence become able to see that the problem is not so much choosing the wrong person over and over again but dancing the same dance over and over again with whomever is willing to be a partner. The DREAM Sequence helps us understand why we are invested in repeating the same routine and gives us techniques for learning how to make different choices.

The following questions address some of the basic concepts you'll explore as you move through the book and represent an overview of the irrelationship-related issues tackled by the DREAM Sequence. These concepts are illustrated in depth with stories, techniques, and experiential processes to help you identify how you're affected by irrelationship and build a solid foundation of awareness and knowledge for change and recovery.

- What does my song-and-dance routine look like and do for me?
- Am I the Performer or the Audience in my routine?
- Why did I originally create this song-and-dance routine, and what benefits did I get from it?
- How did my childhood song-and-dance routine set me up for unsatisfying adult relationships?
- What would be the risks and benefits of abandoning my song-and-dance routine?

The DREAM Sequence helps you grow beyond your contrived song-and-dance routine into free, loving relationships. You'll uncover your irrelationship storyline and the role you play in your song-and-dance routine. This will help you understand:

- why being with you partner feels like a struggle;
- why you often feel as if you're on the outside looking in; and
- why this seems to happen every time you get involved with someone.

Another discovery you'll make is that irrelationship distances you not only from anxiety but also from *all* of your feelings, which makes you unable to enjoy most of the good things relationships have to offer. But the DREAM Sequence will show you that what you've always done doesn't have to be the last word.

Using This Book

As you may have already noticed, the words "Performer" and "Audience" have been capitalized throughout the text. This has been done purposely to maintain clarity in analyzing the irrelationship dynamic.

The book has five sections that build on one another, so they should be read in order to prevent confusion.

- **Part One: Irrelationship on Stage—Your Song-and-Dance Routine** introduces the basic anatomy of irrelationship and helps you build acceptance and patience with yourself as you explore the ways you undermine your chances at love and intimacy.

- **Part Two: Getting to Know You—Spotlight on the Performer and the Audience** profiles the key players of irrelationship. It explores how anxiety drives the players into their song-and-dance routine and reveals the isolation and frustration of trying to maintain safety inside a dysfunctional system.

- **Part Three: Backstage—The Inner Workings of Irrelationship** delves into the core reasons irrelationship developed in the first place and discusses familiar pitfalls that result from staying stuck in the irrelationship pattern for long periods.

- **Part Four: Raising the Curtain on Recovery—From Irrelationship to Real Relationship** introduces the DREAM Sequence of recovery, outlining the five-step process of recognizing and escaping irrelationship.

- **Part Five: Encore—Cracked Open for Love** offers guidance and support for staying on track in recovery.

Each chapter is followed by a series of exercises called Toward Positive Change. These exercises include reflection on your own experience and questions designed to help you apply the ideas in the chapter.

Use a blank journal for writing your reflections and answering the questions. Taking quiet, unhurried time for the work is vital for using the material effectively. Your written answers and reflections are useful for tracking changes in your thinking and behavior.

Create a list of the parts of the book, citing the page number, that resonate with your experience and irrelationship storyline. You'll find validation, relief, and even laughter as you identify with the people and stories presented. Identification of this type is a powerful mechanism for healing, so savor and reflect on it. Whenever you have doubts about the value and direction of your work, revisit earlier parts of your journal to re-orient yourself about where you've been and where you're going.

Welcome to recovery! Get ready for a leap into a process of learning how to live a life of fulfillment and true connection with others.

Part One
Irrelationship on Stage

Your Song-and-Dance Routine

Chapter 1

Anatomy of Irrelationship

Consider the following relationship descriptors. Do any of them resonate with you?

- Do you think you can save, fix, or rescue the person you are drawn to?
- Do you hope that person can fix, save, or rescue you?
- Is your idea of love mostly about taking care of your partner?
- Is your idea of love mostly about your partner taking care of you?
- Do you feel a lack of empathy or reciprocity when you are busy doing things for the person you love?
- When you show you really care, do you feel drained, used, or depleted instead of invigorated?
- Does your relationship often feel like more work than play and more unspoken discomfort than joy?
- Do you feel your relationship is ultimately not enriching your life?

If you answer yes to any of the above questions, it suggests that you may build relationships for all the wrong reasons. But stay with us: you are building awareness, which is an important first step. Also, don't blame yourself for this kind of behavior; this is a pattern you've come by honestly. The fact is, our culture supports one-directional caregiving. It is considered virtuous and makes us so-called good family members, good neighbors, and good citizens. But chronic, one-directional caretaking is actually a dysfunctional pattern learned as infants or small children in the earliest months and years of our relationship with our primary caregiver, usually a parent.[1] In this pattern, we sought to elicit behaviors we needed in order for us to feel safe. These formative transactions were the beginning of a life-long pattern of interactions whose purpose was, and continues into adulthood to be, to manage relationships so that they sustain feelings of safety above all else. Irrelationship is a straitjacket built for two that does not allow a flow of spontaneous loving, but it does protect, at least superficially, against feelings of anxiety. Irrelationship is the ultimate defense. And the attempt to feel safe and anxiety free can trump any kind of authentic loving. However, no matter how much we want to love, over time, the underlying hidden anxiety pushes us to repeat the pattern chronically, so that we never learn how to form real relationships of genuine intimacy and reciprocity. Instead, we live in isolation, even though our lives appear to be actively engaged with others whom we regard as our closest associates, friends, partners, or spouses.

Yet, isolation has a pay-off; it allows us to maintain a safe, non-vulnerable artificiality at the level of emotional investment, free of the risks that come with intimacy. However, the space in which we do interact with others must be filled with something, and that something is called a song-and-dance routine. Briefly, the routine is a set of behaviors, which can be active, passive, or interactive, featuring two people who secretly agree to displace the possibility of authentic interaction between each other. This dynamic of routines—usually designed to resemble caregiving—is, in fact, the opposite of being loving, caring, or giving. By refusing to accept what others around us have to offer, we tend to devalue them. This is an essential marker of irrelationship.

Who Is Who?—The Performer and the Audience

The components of a song-and-dance routine are choreographed to sustain irrelationship. The Performer *overtly* delivers care to the Audience, while the Audience *covertly* administers care to the Performer by pretending the

Performer's part in the routine is desirable and helpful. Thus the Performer sees him- or herself as the giver who administers care to the Audience, while the Audience, appearing to accept what the Performer offers, appears to be the receiver of the Performer's ministrations. The behavior of both, however, is deliberately constructed to block the possibility of a genuine, reciprocal connection. The missing connection prevents the development of shared experience enjoyed in authentic relationships. Each participant's role devalues the other by refusing to validate anything genuine he or she has to offer. Perhaps the most insidious aspect of the irrelationship is that each party experiences isolation and a vague dissatisfaction with the other. Both know on some level that something essential is missing.

Irrelationship as a Survival Tool

Irrelationship is not the result of a failure on the part of either party. In fact, irrelationship is better described as a survival technique that gradually developed in a child who continues to use it in later years. As small children, we experienced the world as unstable, frightening, and sometimes hostile. This experience of instability, however, was actually generated by our caregiver's emotional state—depression, anxiety, unhappiness, or other negative emotion—and made him or her unable to provide conditions that made us feel secure. To manage our anxiety, we used the skills at our disposal to create a song-and-dance routine that we hoped would make our caregiver feel better so that we could feel safe. Flipping roles, we became our parent's caregiver: Julie brought ice packs to her mother in bed or massaged her feet; Liam tried to be funny and make his mom laugh; and Stanley listened quietly while his father complained about his boss. We did whatever our parents' cues told us to do, hoping it would change their mood. When it worked—when their emotional state improved—we felt safe again and could relax.

As can be seen from these examples, the child's routine may be that of either Performer or Audience, but sometimes it may include elements of both. In any case, the child is providing care that enables the ineffective caregiver to believe he or she is a good parent.

19

Having learned as children that our song-and-dance routines worked, we took them forward through our lives and used them whenever necessary to make those around us feel better and ourselves safer. Relating to others in this way is a project doomed from the start; it sets up situations that allow only emotionally guarded interactions that are neither open nor spontaneous and leave no space for sharing, closeness, or intimacy. In fact, the routines stifle awareness of actual human needs and prevent our learning how to meet those needs. Ironically, these routines establish and sustain a defensive dynamic—irrelationship—between parties that does not address the deep, perceived lack of safety, even in close relationships. Whether we're acting as Performer or as Audience, neither touches the other meaningfully to relieve that unease.

Part of the deception of irrelationship is that it feels right, which is a clue that something is badly wrong. It's comfortable because it's numbing, although it looks real from the outside. The participants have unconsciously, but deliberately, chosen to protect themselves from participating meaningfully in the lives of one another. Therefore, use of irrelationship results in a "no winner, no loser" situation.

In abusive relationships, one participant exercises more power than the other, resulting in a winner and a loser. In couples affected by irrelationship, neither participant wins; both participants' anxiety keeps them emotionally locked down. The joint investment in this mechanism is called *brainlock*. Brainlock is an emotional logjam in which nothing gets in and nothing gets out. Both participants selectively ignore the same things together. Most significantly, they ignore the fact that they are using a false connection with one another to defend against intimacy. It can be compared to two people who bury a treasure and then forget where they've buried it.

This doesn't mean that when Performer and Audience interact nothing is going on between them. Their defensive constructs are interlocked so firmly that when they go into recovery, their most challenging task is to step back far enough from their anxiety to allow them to see that the song-and-dance routine they've created has been a stand-in for *genuine* caring behavior.

Sam and Claire's Irrelationship Storyline

Two wannabe stars, Sam and Claire, met one another under the bright lights of New York's Broadway theater world. Each of them sought to escape the unhappiness of failed former relationships. They were immediately attracted to one another, sharing a sense of familiarity and instant comfort. They joined their lives to love and support each other as they made their way toward stardom—at least that is what they thought. And it partly worked.

Sam succeeded in making it on Broadway. Claire's less dramatic success in Off-Off-Broadway productions meant keeping her day job while continuing to struggle on the periphery of show business. After a short time, they began to question their love. They became uneasy with one another and began to act out an obvious song-and-dance routine. The question was, who would be the Performer, the overt caretaker, and who would be the receptive Audience? Before long, the exciting promise of healthy connection slid into the abyss of irrelationship. And because they were actors, their song-and-dance roles became exaggerated. Eventually, they sought couples' therapy.

From the first session, Sam came on larger-than-life as the Performer. He ranted and raved, rarely sitting down. He expected Claire to play the role of adoring Audience, watching him strut on stage, which was their silently-agreed upon script. Sam bragged about how much he did at home and at work—paying the bills, organizing activities and, generally, catering to Claire's every need. In therapy, he made it obvious that he believed all the heavy lifting was necessary to keep their relationship on track.

Claire seemed to be an unappreciative and even disrespectful Audience. She mutely, but ostentatiously, knitted during session while Sam congratulated himself. When Claire remained quiet during Sam's pauses for breath, he'd shout accusingly, "You just don't get it, Claire!" and redoubled his performance, finally shouting, "What about me?" Claire, still knitting, would admit that Sam took care of her and thanked him for it, but she remained withholding and passive.

What was going on? Clearly, Sam was driven, but, just as clearly, Claire never affirmed that Sam's actions contributed anything of value to their shared life. This continued for some months, until one day their therapist told Sam, "You need to stop being so selfish."

Sam was aghast—speechless. The therapist continued, "Yes, it's true—you give and give and give until it hurts you and everyone around you. You give with a vengeance without *allowing* anyone else to contribute—to do anything that has an impact on you. And the message is simple: No one is allowed to believe that anything he or she has to offer is worthwhile—especially Claire. And it's all because down deep you believe that if you don't hold things together, the whole world will fall apart. Living this way has put you in an isolation that neither Claire nor anyone else can penetrate."

Sam was caught red-handed in his song-and-dance routine. Fortunately for both him and Claire, the road to recovery began that moment. Sam was so burned out that he was ready to accept what he was told. He could see and admit to both controlling and suppressing all Claire's attempts to care for him. This enabled him to take the first steps in the frightening but rewarding process of creating a relationship in which he and Claire could trade places, take risks, and learn to care for each other.

Performers are always on the lookout for a work-in-progress to focus on—preferably indefinitely. For Sam, Claire's behavior and passivity was like job security. Claire's non-stellar theater career was full of frustration and disappointment that Sam could fix without having to examine what was going on between them. Sam's enthusiasm for caretaking blocked his self-awareness, giving Claire opportunity to enjoy the passive-aggressive pleasure of playing victim while denying Sam the gratification of successfully fixing her. This careful arrangement satisfied their need to ignore how emotionally distanced they had become from one another.

At first, all Claire had to do was passively act as if her partner's routines were helping her. Although their song-and-dance routines were strikingly dissimilar, they shared a major trait: both were highly invested in fixing, saving, or rescuing someone important to them.

Sam first learned his routine as a child when he devised a series of performances for his depressed mother to make her feel better. Conversely, Claire's routine was to act as if her detached mother and father gave good performances as parents. Both performances were designed to relieve household anxiety. Unfortunately, neither of their caregiving compulsions ended when they left home. Instead, they took their unconscious need to be helpers with them, chronically repeating the pattern, unaware of being driven by a need to keep the world from falling apart.

Once Sam and Claire shared their storylines with one another, they felt as if they had shared intimacy for the first time in years. They began to see how they administered the same treatment to one another that they had used on their parents.

Although the story of Sam and Claire may seem extreme, partnerships like this are common. With some couples, when conflict develops, one partner becomes increasingly convinced he or she is the injured party while the other feigns passive innocence. Angry but unopposed, the active partner begins to make a noose for the passive partner but at the last minute hangs him- or herself after being rejected by the other as a failed caregiver. The Audience's investment is so deep that he or she practically kicks the chair from under the gallows and sits back to enjoy the spectacle.

Claire maintained her safety by letting Sam be her hero-rescuer who would take responsibility for everything in their relationship. That way, no matter how messy things got, fingers could be pointed only in his direction.

But Claire's posture was no less isolating than Sam's fix-it routine. When at length she became unwilling to pretend that Sam's performing did her any good, the show devolved into dreary melodrama. Claire wasn't aggressive: she merely refused to invest herself or to validate Sam. Consequently, the anxiety their song-and-dance routine was designed to circumvent surfaced with a vengeance. By the time they started therapy, Sam saw himself as an almost abusively unappreciated caregiver, while Claire had completely lost interest.

As their therapy went forward, Sam and Claire unfolded the backstory of their fear of intimacy. As they did so, they were surprised to find themselves recovering the excitement of their early relationship. Piece by piece, they disassembled the anxiety that caused them to invest in irrelationship and began building a life of genuine intimacy.

Where Have You Been All My Life?

Irrelationship brings people together in interlocking, scripted roles for all the wrong reasons. Primed by histories created by irrelationship, they learn to identify one another by unconscious pattern recognition and set themselves up to fall almost instantly into a song-and-dance routine. Instead of a measured but exciting courtship, the two partners meet, fall for one another, and "mate for life" in the space of a few days. Early sexual contact elevates bonding hormones for both parties—either driving them apart, resulting in a series of one-night stands, or abandoning or cementing the relationship prematurely. Before either can stop, consider, and perhaps, separate, they jump in with both feet almost instantly. This causes the couple to miss red flags seen by others—or perhaps by themselves. What they're attracted to in each other—commitment to the song-and-dance routine—ultimately becomes their undoing. Burdened with unrecognized or unnamed dissatisfactions, resentment builds. Esteem is undermined by refusal to allow mutual contribution. Intimacy is thwarted, making the entire construct liable to collapse under the right stressors.

Irrelationship becomes effective between persons who, even before they meet, agree to be "exactly who you need me to be" provided "you will do the same for me." But how do they find one another in the first place? Many people complain that they experience the same relationship disappointments repeatedly, finding a partner who will act out the sought-after role-play until it burns out. This addictive pattern continues to rule their choices until they become able to identify it and the part they play in it.

Across a Crowded Room

As you read this scenario, look for anything that might look or sound like your own experience.

*I see you across the room. I sense, I feel, in my heart some special unfathomable, for-my-eyes-only, X-factor that distinguishes you from all others. Chemistry. I'm already forgetting myself. I've promised myself I would **not** meet someone this* *way again after what happened the last twelve times. But I want you. I don't know why, but I am driven toward you. I need to know who you are and find out if you, at last, are who I've been looking for.*

In irrelationship terms, this scenario means, "I am drawn to you because you have that secret neediness that I was born to fix, just as I have the type of neediness that draws you to me. Somehow, on an intuitive level, my brain knows. That small child's habit learned long ago has hijacked my will, leading me eagerly to my doom like the Siren's song, enticing sailors toward the rocks."

And so, I feel this desire as I come toward you. I reach out and introduce myself. And, while I feel that I want you, that I must have you, I also sense an unbridgeable gap between us.

Research into gambling behavior has shown that near misses increase the drive behind a gambler's compulsive, reward-seeking behavior.[2] This happens via brain mechanisms that measure external situations and produce activation in the ventral tegmental areas of the brain and other areas related to pleasure and decision-making.[3] For example, when playing slot machines, four out of five cherries makes a person more likely to continue playing than hitting only three out of five cherries, thinking, *Damn it. I almost got it that time! Just one more round! Just one!*

Psychologically, almost getting it makes people think—incorrectly—that they have a better chance of getting what they want if they keep trying because, after all, last time they "almost got it." In the emotional and reward-based reactions, they lose touch with the ability to see that the chance of winning has nothing to do with the previous outcome. Similarly, connections driven by irrelationship delude us into believing that a near miss improves the likelihood that "next time will be different."

I reach for you—and you slip through my fingers (even though you may be playing out a similar scenario in your head). My heart aches for you. I ask you for a date. Even if you say yes, our union is impossible—it has to be. I reach and I reach for you. My desire is unbearable—and the game itself, while killing me, is also thrilling me. But if I get what I think I want, if I succeed, my desire will drain away. I must have you. I must fix you or you must fix me—and, no matter how much you try to convince me that you are mine, I somehow don't catch you. And anyway, what would be the fun in actually catching you? No, I want this cat-and-mouse game to go on indefinitely.[4]

The entire dynamic for this scenario is fueled by the notion of drive rather than mere desire. Something drives the irrelationship process: the need for security, the need to believe that we live in a safe world, a world that is not falling apart. Deep within the anxiety driving irrelationship is the terror that we will not be able to maintain safety unless we keep the world stable. And this drive will continue indefinitely.

I'm drawn to you—driven to repeat the irrelationship pattern with you. Both of us are possessed by the same need that took shape when we were children. We're conspirators dancing a routine that will protect us from the dangers of the world—especially the threat of intimacy and unbridled feelings that each represents to the other. So instead of risking reality, let's dance—all night if we have to.

Rocking the Boat

Do you find contact with loved ones and others to be enriching, flowing, and vital? Or, are you troubled by a vague feeling that something isn't right about your connection with others—perhaps even that true connection is completely missing?

Are you in a relationship in which you are either a Performer like Sam or an Audience like Claire? Maybe you're vaguely aware of using a song-and-dance routine like theirs to meet unspoken needs, remaining detached as you go about your business, afraid to rock the boat and risk disturbing the balance between you. No matter who you are in the song-and-dance routine, both parties are trapped by a need to exclude give-and-take, ignore ups and downs, and, above all, hide vulnerability.

The detached "non-feeling" of irrelationship is usually experienced as depression. But the depression is actually a cover for a psychological defense known as *dissociation*—a state in which all experience is whitewashed so everything feels much like everything else.[5] This is another aspect of the protective function of irrelationship that keeps us safe from exposing our hearts to the risk of losing someone we perceive as valuable. The depression-like dissociative state short-circuits any anxiety connected with the risk of loss. Many of us have begun relationships that looked like they worked until they disintegrated, sometimes in terrible ways. And yet we do it again and again, seduced by romantic stories and images from movies, television, literature, songs, and opera, all promising that just the right fit is out there. But once again we find out that Mr. Right wasn't so right, and Ms. Perfect wasn't so perfect after all.

Toward Positive Change

Open your journal and let's get started.

1. List ways in which you have acted as a caregiver for your parents, both as a child and an adult. Write brief descriptions and details from specific episodes.

2. What did you believe you accomplished by helping your parents as a child? How did success feel at the time? Did success last or did you have to step in repeatedly?

3. Think about ways in which you have acted as a caregiver for other significant people in your life—other family members, coworkers, friends, and past lovers. Describe each briefly, including what the person needed and what you did to help.

4. Do you have a connection in your life—romantic or otherwise—that seems to have the characteristics of irrelationship? Looking back on your acquaintanceship with that person, explain what initially drew you to that person. Then describe what didn't work out as you had hoped.

Chapter 2

Performer or Audience?

Both the Performer and the Audience share the fear that the world is going to fall apart if he or she doesn't do something to fix or save the caretaker. Although the methods are different, both Performer and Audience are motivated by fear and anxiety.

Performers tend to use intrusive, self-centered maneuvers in their caretaking—planned actions whose real purpose is self-protection. Aggression, of course, can show itself in passive as well as active forms. The Audience may operate in a passive-aggressive manner at the expense of the Performer, who is generally determined to stand out as the active member of the relationship but is usually unwilling be cast as the bad guy by the Audience—at least not explicitly.[1] The Performer actively pursues fix-it activities that allow the Audience to hide in the role of non-participant or even victim. From that position, the Audience can passively punish the Performer by not responding to treatment, namely by not feeling better. In reality, however, few cases are this black-and-white.

A more typical pattern emerges when two people are caught up in conflict, and the Performer, seeing him- or herself as the injured party, acts out by criticizing and blaming the Audience. In this type of scenario, the Audience provides space for the Performer by deliberately assuming a passive posture. After their relationship collapses, the Audience consoles him- or herself by believing this is the natural consequence of getting involved with a personality so aggressive that it can't be controlled.

Ready, Aim, Backfire!

What does the dialogue between a Performer and an Audience sound like when they are brainlocked in a blame-game? Let's take a closer look at an exchange between Performer Laurie and her Audience husband Lou.

Laurie: Your secrets are killing me, Lou; they're killing us. I cannot believe after all I've done for you and all I keep doing for this family, you can just sit there and say nothing. How can you be so completely unwilling to tell me what you have been up to? I've tried and I've tried—I've done everything. What else can I do?

Lou: [silence]

Laurie: The more I do for you, the more you shut down. The more I ask from you, the more you disappear. What's wrong? How in the world can I possibly make things any better between us?

Lou: [silence]

Laurie: How can you just sit there saying nothing? I really believed that when I took on that second job, when I started teaching again, when I, at great personal cost to me, supported you on your new business venture and found more childcare and then wound up taking on more care of our son, you'd finally see how much I do, how much I've done for you—for us.

Lou: I do.

Laurie: Then why won't you tell me what you're up to all day? With all that I do for you, Lou, why should I have to worry about what you're doing? Why do I have to be the one who does it all—and still feel like the bad guy?

Lou: I know how much you do for me—for us. I know we would not have made it through these difficult times without everything you've done. And I thank you.

Laurie: Well, well! Thank you.

Lou: [silence]

With the expertise of these irrelationship veterans, both Laurie and Lou were able to thwart yet another opportunity for intimacy—or the threat of intimacy. Although their roles are dramatically different, this example demonstrates how their agreed-upon roles collaborate with a single purpose. And most of all, they clearly built this routine together.

The observant eye might notice that while Lou quietly acknowledges, and even applauds, Laurie's contributions, he resists any obligation they might place on him—especially commitment to what might be otherwise considered their joint purpose in taking care of their family. He keeps to the sidelines allowing Laurie to take all the responsibility or blame for what is right and what is wrong in their life together.

"After all I've done for you," is this type of Performer's refrain. The Audience's role provides lukewarm acknowledgement and applause—a lame stand-in for silence.

As we can see, the Audience is an exceptionally hard target, which is actually the point. Lou has allowed Laurie to take all the responsibility for the relationship while he emotionally slips out the back door, leaving Laurie unaware of why she feels lonely, suspicious, and afraid. Lou's silence reinforces Laurie's performance in a scenario in which his actual presence is not required. Caretaking provided and interaction avoided. Mission accomplished.

Stuck in the Song-and-Dance Routine

Sometimes what appears beneficial—the "feel-good" parts of doing the song-and-dance routine—are so compelling that getting out of it isn't nearly as appealing as staying in it. If you are the Performer, it's heady to be told by others that you're like a mind reader; you seem to know what your Audience is feeling even before he or she does. Who wouldn't like being described as selfless, sensitive to others, and always ensuring others' needs are met? It sometimes feels like a full-time job, but the payoff in admiration and praise feels great, right?

And wouldn't it be wonderful, as the Audience, to find "the one who understands" you? The partner who is so crazy about you that he or she's continually anticipating your needs and taking care of them, sometimes almost before you're aware of them? A partner who always has solutions and is so smart, funny, helpful and fun to be with? When you're with that person you feel alive and full of hope. Now your life is going to be right. He or she will take care of you forever and will never hurt you. And all you have to do is be yourself. Yes, sometimes it can be tiring; and other times this person is a little quick to tell you about your needs and shortcomings, but nobody's perfect.

Well, if it's all that good, why is it falling apart? Come to think of it, haven't you been here before? Didn't the last promising relationship come crashing down—and the one before that? In the beginning, everything was perfect: Each of you knew your expected parts and seemed to be excited about playing them together. So what was the signal—who said or did what—that made one or both of you sense danger?

Stopping the Song-and-Dance Routine

Realizing that irrelationship is not the answer is great news because it means love, hatred, fear, and joy are still alive. But this isn't just a matter of becoming aware of denied or hidden feelings. Mutually collaborative relationships in which both parties feel safe talking about their feelings is usually scary, especially at first. But once the awkwardness passes, it feels right and even good. Rather than distancing from feelings for fear that they will prove to be uncontrollable, exploring feelings together becomes the beginning of true and mutually rewarding intimacy.

Using the schema below, review the dynamics of irrelationship to determine which role, or roles, you play in the song-and-dance routine. You'll know who you are. Be honest but without self-criticism.

Features of Irrelationship

PERFORMER

Give, give, give—until it hurts.

Characteristics: Builds resentment, anxiety, acting out, and imbalance; has feelings of superiority, emotional distance, and false sense of safety; contrives giving behaviors; devalues others.

+

AUDIENCE

Take, take, take—until it hurts.

Characteristics: Impenetrability, anxiety, and acting out; fakes it to make routines appear effective; intentionally foils partner's efforts to help, fix, and rescue; defends against accepting what others offer.

=

IRRELATIONSHIP

Emotional distance or absence, which defends against empathy, intimacy, emotional risk, and emotional investment.

Outcomes: Depression, dissociation, and isolation

Toward Positive Change

The following questions and exercises will help you identify parts of Lou and Laurie's story that resonate with you.

1. Are you the Performer or the Audience—or do you mix both roles?

2. What personal traits or behaviors give you away as Performer or Audience? How do they show up in your interactions with others?

3. What situations or feelings trigger your song-and-dance routine?

4. What are the benefits of your song-and-dance routine? What is it like to identify and observe yourself performing these behaviors?

5. Now as an adult, what ways can you deal with relationship-based anxiety that you couldn't as a child?

Chapter 3

Short-Circuiting the Possibility of Love

Irrelationship is a psychological defense system that drives counterfeit connections and, on the surface, looks like real relationship.

The child Performer was driven to always be "on." Conversely, the child Audience was always driven to be "there," to be attentive. The budding, compulsive caregiver is always ready to create and sustain the delusion of self-sufficiency. The initial benefit of this pattern is that it allows the individual, now an adult, to make a deal with anxiety. However, the long-term effect is that the adult has unknowingly borrowed against future security, creating emotional debt without knowing how high the principal and the interest are going to be. But this isn't the type of debt that, once paid off, disappears from the ledger. Instead, the borrower goes through life locked in irrelationship with every new encounter.

To shield themselves from awareness of this conflict, people caught in irrelationship use a powerful psychological defense known as *dissociation*. Dissociation protects us from the awareness, but not from the effects, of traumatizing experience. Pain, although numbed, or dissociated, doesn't go away. Unfortunately, the effects of dissociation go even deeper; avoiding pain (or conflict) becomes a primary characteristic of how we live our lives.

The song-and-dance routine is a visible aspect of this encoding and becomes our unvarying means of relating to the world. A comparison can be made to a neurological disorder that causes constant, involuntary physical movements or to a puppeteer pulling our strings and forcing us repeatedly to act out the role of Performer or Audience.

Participants in irrelationship threaten each other with the risks inherent in empathy, intimacy, emotional connection, and emotional investment. To manage this threat, Performer and Audience jointly create *brainlock*, a state that excludes the possibility of give-and-take or sharing of experience.

By taking a look at Glen and Vicky's story, we can better understand how anxiety and delusion can underlie irrelationship.

Glen and Vicky's Connection

Glen met Vicky in graduate school. As Glen described their first meeting, he said, "I felt something knock me on my head, throw me over its shoulder, and drag me off to the land of love that, by then, I'd come to believe could only exist in a fantasy. It just felt so right."

Certainly our culture's take on romance set up Glen for thinking that he found the right person. At last, his life would be perfect. He often wondered to himself what it was that made Vicky feel so familiar. He would say, "It's just so easy to be myself when I'm with her." He had no way of knowing he'd been kicked in the head by his own brain, which had been programmed for this kind of delusion when he was too young to understand what was happening.

According to Glen, their dating began with a blaze of rewarding and intense sexual attraction and bonding. Their hormonally mediated excitement shielded them from the less pleasant aspects of their relational reality. Soon they were swearing true love to one another, something Glen had done repeatedly at the beginning of his relationships with women. For both Glen and Vicky, however, this was the real deal. Passionate lovemaking, adventurous travel, and visits to their families—pleased that they had finally found someone—confirmed their devotion, along with shared dreams.

Why wouldn't Glen love Vicky? She laughed at his jokes and told him he was brilliant and made her feel happy. Listening to his stories, Vicky related to the struggles that led to Glen's choice of a career in clinical psychology, which was also her profession.

And why wouldn't Vicky love Glen? He understood her, was sensitive and patient, and went to great lengths to reach her when she was emotionally distressed. They had so much in common that it was easy to see how they were deceived into believing each had found a lost part of themselves.

Glen enjoyed seeing Vicky as an emotional labyrinth that he alone could navigate. Somehow, he knew he could fix her—whether or not she felt that she needed fixing. Being with Vicky made Glen feel secure, powerful, and irreplaceable. And Glen made Vicky believe that she could finally feel alive. What could be wrong with this picture? In roles so well paired—he the Performer and she the Audience—why wouldn't they be a match made in heaven? Wouldn't their complementary roles lead to a durable, exciting marriage that provided fulfillment to both of them?

The truth, however, proved to be something quite different; they were building and feeding irrelationship, quickly moving from a simulation of intimacy to a chilly isolation. Ultimately they found themselves at odds, firmly defended against what the other offered.

Glen sought psychoanalysis for himself, partly because he was considering adding psychoanalytic training to his credentials. Having hit a wall in his practice, he hoped the analytical process and training program would help him to discover the reason for his growing sense that his clinical practice was stagnating. He was beginning to resent that his patients weren't getting better, although in some cases they seemed increasingly dependent on him even though they disparaged both his work and himself personally. He was beginning to wonder if his patients were punishing him for trying to help them get well, or, passive-aggressively, by not getting well. Reflecting on this a few months into his marriage to Vicky, Glen remarked, "I've sometimes felt the same way about my wife." Neither spouse acknowledged how brittle their relationship had become but were brainlocked into maintaining it, even though each felt a deep trepidation about it.

As Glen explored his history of playing the Performer for his wife and others in his past, he began to articulate the dynamics of what he came to understand as irrelationship—his taking on the role of caretaker in his professional role and in his marriage. But his assuming the caretaker role began years before when Glen, the young Performer, treated his mother's extreme sadness and disappointment by playing the young jokester, attempting to lift her spirits whenever he could.

Glen described his mother and father as "children of the '60s," and they were married very young. When Glen was born, they were both eighteen years old. His mother came from a wealthy family while his father was a "boy from the wrong side of the tracks." A premarital pregnancy and their marriage were provocative and taken as insulting to his mother's family, who expected children to be seen and not heard. Soon after their marriage, Glen's father enlisted in the Army and served in Vietnam where he found alcohol, heroin, prostitutes, and post-traumatic stress. During the same period, Glen's mother found born-again Christianity. Notwithstanding Jesus, Glen's mother became deeply depressed. Her depression was the impetus for Glen to learn his basic song-and-dance routine of slapstick humor, jokes, and tricks that seemed to relieve the cloud that hung over the household.

When Glen's father returned from Vietnam, the marriage fell apart quickly. His mother fantasized that she would be able to fix her husband with religion, but he left instead. This pressed Glen into increasing his caretaking of his mother. Always "on," he maniacally performed for her, doing his routine anywhere he could. And it often worked. All through school he continued his song-and-dance routine, becoming known as the class clown. He was undeniably popular and people apparently liked him, but he never felt significantly connected to any of his classmates. They might enjoy being around him, but close friendships eluded him. In fact, the closer he seemed to come to anyone—especially women to whom he was romantically attracted—the more easily he would resent them. And the feeling became mutual. At the end of his unsuccessful romantic relationships, his girlfriends uniformly complained that he didn't really seem to value them, which Glen found confusing and unfair.

Perhaps the best example of a romantic partner (and soon to be Audience) whom Glen ultimately devalued was his wife Vicky. When they met in graduate school, Glen's routines seemed to make Vicky feel better. The reason is easy to understand; early in their relationship she revealed details of her childhood that motivated her to become a therapist. But her song-and-dance routine, which she originally devised to treat her mother and father, was the opposite of Glen's routine. Through her childhood, Vicky created ways to make her neglectful parents believe that they were good parents—although she actually believed her mother was unbalanced and her father incompetent.

The darker reaches of Vicky's backstory were quite different from Glen's. Her mother married the high school football star in their small southwestern town. The fact that he was a bit of a cowboy made it even better; her mom had grown up romanticizing the Old West. Unfortunately the starry-eyed days were short-lived, and her football-star husband ended up in the unromantic job of a car salesman, while Vicky's mother started her own successful business. Two children were born, a boy and Vicky, who learned while still very young to be their mother's Audience. Vicky's earliest memories were of listening to unending stories in which her mother was "star of the show," but as she got older, her mother's behavior became increasingly bizarre and destructive. Vicky, meanwhile, continued to pretend that her mother and father were good parents—a farce Vicky's brother refused to validate. She continued the charade but when time came for her to go to college, she fled the Southwest for New York City.

Although their stories are strikingly dissimilar, Vicky and Glen clearly shared a major trait: They were highly invested in helping, i.e., fixing, curing, or rescuing those who were significant in their lives, whether or not these figures were seen as loved ones. Glen's song-and-dance routine was a series of performances directed at making his depressed mother feel happy. Conversely, Vicky's song-and-dance routine was to play the Audience, pretending her mother and father were good parents.

Neither of their caregiving compulsions ended when Glen and Vicky left their families of origin. They took their unconscious need to be "help-a-holics" into many or most of their future relationships. By chronically repeating this caregiving pattern, they were unaware that they were motivated by their desperate need to keep the world from falling apart. When Glen and Vicky met and became one another's new family, they recreated their old family dynamics with some minor adjustments, while retaining the destructive dynamics.

Glen and Vicky are two textbook examples of loving for all the wrong reasons. In both their cases, keeping the world from falling apart was the reason for loving. But, their marriage pact had nothing to do with love; it was an unspoken agreement to marginalize the possibility—and risk—of genuine investment in one another. Instead, they proceeded through life in silence about either of their unmet needs, thereby eliminating the possibility of thriving and change.

Even though Glen and Vicky told their stories to one another, this paradoxically (and deceptively) failed to establish intimacy between them. Vicky retained emotional reserve and made no explicit claims upon Glen as to her place in his life. Their stories remained separate. Brainlock prevented the possibility that each could function in the other's life other than how they had always functioned. Neither Glen nor Vicky could listen to or empathize with the other, which made it impossible for them to create and share a life together.

Vicky's caretaking performance for Glen—similar to the care she administered to her parents—was simply to accept Glen's treatment. For his part, having come to experience Vicky as cold and sexless, Glen redoubled his song-and-dance routine. And for a time it seemed to work; Glen got the same satisfaction he received from making his depressed mother smile. Deep inside, however, Glen knew that the whole relationship was a ruse; he was not happy and became aware of a vague anxiety about the future.

A couple of years after they were married, the reality behind Glen's expectations of his irrelationship with his wife became clear. While he and his analyst uncovered the dynamics in his caretaking role, Glen attempted to share his crisis with Vicky, appealing to her for support and empathy, but she withdrew—emotionally at first but ultimately to the point where Glen realized he was living with someone who was not just unavailable but unknown to him. He was forced to face the reality that Vicky had no interest in being a companion in any of his life crises. From Vicky's side, the agreement to be Glen's Audience included the unspoken proviso that if the going ever got rough, she would get going, just as she did when she left her childhood home.

Through this turn of events, the nature of the irrelationship became clear to Glen and to his analyst. His connection with Vicky was isolating, stultifying, and filled with resentment. Vicky's bright-eyed receptivity to Glen's routine was revealed as *her* fantasy-based routine. At that moment, Glen woke up and began the process of finally looking seriously at his history as a Performer, facing how he had unconsciously depended upon his song-and-dance routine to short-circuit any approach of closeness in relationships.

Deeper Analysis and Some Brain Science

As we can see again in Glen and Vicky's story, the behaviors associated with irrelationship are designed to defend against anxiety. But just what *is* anxiety? Anxiety is the initial reaction of a sensitive system that is wired to keep us vigilant to danger and to protect us from harm.[1] Everyone experiences anxiety and finds ways of managing it. When anxiety is managed well, we function better and are happier. But when anxiety is handled in ways that diminish awareness of our feelings, but not the feelings themselves, we lose the guidance of our emotions. This puts us at risk for unhealthy and even dangerous emotional situations. As our denial of anxiety grows and deepens, we are at an ever-increasing risk of being overwhelmed by tidal waves of apparently unintelligible feelings that seem to come out of nowhere.

This psychological adaptation actually results in changes to the structure of the brain and function of brain networks. Our frontal cortex (the higher brain) gets into the habit of ignoring our limbic system (the emotional brain), resulting in a combination of too much *and* too little inhibition, plus a poor sense of timing. Because we never learned the skills needed to deal constructively with emotional crises, we use one of two blunt instruments to handle them: either we use dissociation to numb our feelings, or we explode into rage to crush challenges based on our carefully agreed-upon roles. This is known as *emotional dysregulation* and is essential to maintaining irrelationship. As we saw in attachment theory, two people—who individually have difficulty with emotional regulation within intimate relationships and are emotionally dysregulated—can resort to the mechanisms of irrelationship to create long-term stability.

The bottom line is that no matter how hard we work at convincing ourselves (as Glen and Vicky did) that we are in touch with ourselves, we can, and will, use irrelationship to maintain distance and hide from our feelings. Regardless of the devices we use, our best thinking can't trick our feelings.

When we blind ourselves to our emotions, responding to them authentically is practically impossible. We may want to present ourselves to another person—especially a romantic interest—as a source of strength and support. But if we're putting on an act of always looking strong when we're actually terrified, we're paying the price of not being emotionally present in the relationship. If we've lost a sense of our own emotions and needs, we've lost the ability to reflect and make good decisions even for ourselves. On the other hand, if we believe that what we feel is the only reliable indicator of how things really are (called *emotional reasoning* in cognitive behavioral therapy), we live in a shrunken reality with little space for the joy, excitement, and wisdom that come with spontaneity and space for reflection.

In Glen and Vicky's life of irrelationship, Glen's apparent abundant generosity toward Vicky seemed to be a kind of strength, and Glen was gratified by Vicky's tolerant attention. But Glen and Vicky were trapped by false ideas about themselves and each other that became prisons of isolation and resentment from which both feared escaping.

How Our Brains Make or Shut Down Love

Most people caught in irrelationship have no inkling that anything is wrong until it begins not to work, particularly since it seems to have worked well in the past. Our song-and-dance routines so effectively distract us from our anxiety that we can't imagine anything needs to change. We have no idea how afraid we are and how our unconscious fear disallows change of any kind. Or, equally destructive, our fear drives us to pursue change compulsively and unreflectively without allowing a new person or situation the chance of proving worthwhile. Unsettling as this may be on some level, and may appear to others, the price of shutting down oneself is willingly paid in order to anesthetize anxiety.

While we're doing our song-and-dance routine, the brain continues to produce bonding chemicals. Oxytocin, for example, shifts us into a state of unconditional caring appropriate for a mother caring for a distressed child but lacks the erotic potential driven by testosterone and suppresses dopamine, the brain chemical that mediates many of the pleasurable sensations associated with passionate sexual interaction. In addition, studies of the experience of unconditional love demonstrate that while involved in an intense caretaking role, our brain's capacity for experiencing pain, mediated in the *periaqueductal gray matter,* is muted.[2] This can be seen in a mother caring for her highly vulnerable newborn or sick child. When administering such care, as Performer or Audience, the sensibility of one's own needs and pain are temporarily suspended. Our mind becomes that of the soldier, dancer, yogi, or even the martyr whose single-minded concern is the completion of a task whose significance overrides all other considerations.

Irrelationship thus sidelines large quarters of our emotional life, placing balanced, real relationships out of our reach—whether in business, with friends, or, perhaps especially, with lovers, spouses, or partners. When acting as Performer or Audience, the long-term need to be in healthy, supportive relationships is sacrificed to the immediate imperative of smothering our deep-seated discomfort, thus putting us radically out of balance with others and ourselves. We can live like this for a while, but eventually we crash. At that point, we often become overtly sick and in need of care. The debt has come due and has to be paid back at a high rate of interest.[3]

Toward Positive Change

1. Looking back at your worst romantic relationship, what made it disappointing or a failure?

2. What role did your song-and-dance routine play in that failed relationship? What was your partner's part in the routine? How did each of you prevent closeness from developing?

3. Think about your best relationships in the following areas: family, work, friendship, and romance. What similarities can you identify?

Chapter 4

The Threat of Intimacy

Irrelationship is widespread and subversive. By its nature, it conceals itself, almost hypnotically, confusing and distracting those living within it. Ironically, it clothes itself with language and gestures resembling genuine love and care. We fool ourselves into believing our compulsive caretaking proves how generous and kind we are. This does not mean that, at heart, we are not genuinely inclined toward generosity and kindness. However, our anxiety has hijacked the vocabulary of love, using it instead to manufacture a risk-free space of irrelationship. One aspect of irrelationship is that crucial elements of one's song-and-dance routine become nonnegotiable, such as a rigid need to always be right or an inability to see anything beyond one's own point of view. This is the case with Betty and Hank.

Betty and Hanks' Irrelationship Storyline

"I don't care how bad arguing with me makes you feel, I'm going to win this argument no matter what, because I'm right," said Betty the Performer to her Audience husband Hank.

If being right is part of one's identity as a caregiver, it can easily become more important than the feelings of others, including loved ones. Betty's parents trained her to think that being right was more important for gaining their regard than love and empathy. This type of regard was what they gave to Betty in place of actual love. Performers often fail to recognize this trait because they believe being right is essentially where their goodness or lovability lies—not realizing they learned this harsh attitude toward others in childhood.

"Remind me—what was the argument anyway?" Hank asked. By taking the Audience role, Hank was able to distance himself from accountability—or attack—for what was really going on between them.

At this point, Betty and Hank were so embroiled in arguing that Hank had lost track of the content of their disputes, and he had ceased to even care. This, of course, made Betty feel unappreciated. But Hank had lost the ability to think intelligently and reflectively about what had happened between them.

In terms of brain activity, comparatively automatic parts of Hank's brain took over. He was "brainjacked," so to speak, by areas called the *ventral striatum* and *amygdala*. The ventral striatum codes habit-based learning, or conditioned responses. The amygdala activates when strong emotions are present, stereotypically fear. This results in fight-or-flight reactions and fear-based conditioning. When emotions are well-regulated, two areas together balance out this fear-based conditioning: the *frontal cortex*, which allows for top-down inhibition of strong emotions, letting reason to intervene, and the *hippocampus*, which works in concert with its next door neighbor, the amygdala, to put fear in perspective so it doesn't take over. In Hank's case, caught in the throes of irrelationship, he was on autopilot.

The result was that Hank was the perfect passive Audience for Betty's need to be right. Additionally, she was able to amass even more power through her ability to remember every detail about their arguments. From Betty's perspective, "being right" was the purpose of their relationship. And her ability, as court stenographer, to track their disputes gave her an even greater feeling of superiority.

When Betty and Hank went into couples' therapy, Betty, who had been a magazine editor in a management position, attempted to occupy the therapeutic process in the same way that she had occupied Hank—going so far as to advise the therapist on how to handle their case. Betty's need to control was so stultifying that the therapist even sought supervision to assist her with managing it. Through a difficult process, all three participants had the opportunity to see the power of Betty's need for control, Hank's bewilderment as Audience, and how entrenched both were.

Over time Betty was able to see how their song-and-dance routine kept her from realizing how much she valued and relied on Hank. Hank came to see that he acted out his caring for Betty primarily in his choice to be of service to her by becoming incompetent and needing her help. Even when Betty hit bottom, attempting to fix Hank and going to therapy, her need to be right still protected her from her fear of intimacy with Hank, just as Hank's persona of incompetence allowed him to keep his distance from Betty. Poisonous resentment permeated their irrelationship and over time bubbled inexorably to the surface.

One day in therapy, Betty asked some deeply honest questions that began to shatter the mold of their irrelationship. "What if I have not been right about anything—ever? What does that mean for us? Is the love I thought Hank had for me just some kind of dream? Did I become his wife and caregiver because I thought his loving me depended on it? Do I believe my being right is what holds us together?" Betty had uncovered a *window of opportunity*, a real place to begin to see their shared agreement and actually undo it.

Hank looked up suddenly and said, "Us? There hasn't been an *us* for a long, long time, Betty. And now I'm starting to think I contributed to that far more than I could ever have believed."

As their work progressed, both were able to see that Hank's role as Audience allowed them to keep a safe distance from one another, not risking the conscious emotional investment that is part of intimacy. Betty's need to be right had nothing to do with anything important in their lives; it was only an accessory helping to maintain the space between them. In the act of confronting this, Betty realized that always being right meant being alone. Hank realized he used his incompetence to create the safe but lonely place he had lived in for years.

As Betty and Hank learned to see one another again outside their song-and-dance routine, they remembered how much they cared for each other. As they recovered, they learned how to *be with* each other, as they had never done. And together they learned how to live with and through the anxiety-ridden threat of intimacy without returning to the painful distance of irrelationship.

Wiring the Brain for the Song-and-Dance Routine

Although the Performer may employ a variety of active behaviors, the Audience's posture makes the entire process possible. As can be seen from the case of Hank and Betty, Betty couldn't have acted out her need to be right all the time if Hank hadn't provided space for it. The Performer is emotionally dependent on the willing subordination of the Audience. Hank and Betty's song-and-dance routine was born decades back when they each tried to induce a desired response from their caregivers. Betty practiced being "right and tough." Hank was more actively absent, being out of his caregiver's immediate consciousness.

No matter which behavior surfaces, it is used to allow the caregiver to believe that he or she is a good parent. Once the right song-and-dance routine is formulated, the child can and will use it whenever necessary to feel safe again. The child becomes caregiver to the parent, and the parent accepts the child's ministrations. This is their unspoken agreement. For the child, however, the agreement is struck long before he or she is developmentally capable of comprehending what's happening. The agreement is put into play in the right brain years before the child will have developed the left-brain-based skills to comprehend and integrate it. Consequently, this subliminal technique of negotiating personal safety becomes a driving force in the management of future relationships.

The science of how our brains work explains how this happens. The old, habit-driven, automatic mechanisms in our brains (called the *ventral system*, especially the striatum) dominate our functioning. These mechanisms are simplistic and don't include the ability to examine our responses and actions. In contrast, the parts of our brains that developed later in human evolution (the *dorsal system*) are where more sophisticated functions occur—the capacity for self-reflection and flexibility as well as the ability to evaluate circumstances and situations thoughtfully. However, the case of the child's taking care of the parent is far more complex.

We are born with a rudimentary capacity to empathize, that is, to feel someone else's pain.[1] Without the capacity to analyze and reflect, however, the child is able to react to the pain of others only in terms of how it may impact on him- or herself. As a result, the child is able to interpret the parent's unhappy emotional state only as a threat to his or her own safety. This suggests that the child's capacity for automatic empathy, yet undeveloped capacity for reflection, compassion, and self-regulation, makes him or her liable to amplify the parent's negative emotions. If the parent fails to set healthy boundaries (that is, adhere to the role of parent) the child will be at risk for having unhealthy relationship patterns etched into his or her brain.

The vocabulary of the song-and-dance routine is also determined by the infinite variations in human temperament. But these routines have a lockstep quality in common that excludes discussion or reflection. Once established, the routine unconditionally resists adapting to the complexities of particular relationships. The inability to examine and adapt will cause the affected child to bring this routine into future adult interactions with negative, and sometimes even disastrous, results.

GRAFTS: Variations on Our Song-and-Dance Routine

An infinite variety of patterns of interaction become grafted into a child's personality as a result of experiences from the early childhood environment, particularly the mother, father, and general family system. The familial "dos and don'ts," the cultural norms, the patterns of interaction, and the implicit and explicit needs and desires are instructive and teach the child how he or she must "be" in and with the environment. These factors, as they become expectations, combine with inborn temperament to form the basis for the child's song-and-dance routines.

In the individual affected by irrelationship, these routines developed from childhood interactions with his or her primary caregiver. The song-and-dance routine, the actual interpersonal behavioral routines that get repeated in irrelationship, arise partially from individual attachment style as it inclines toward preoccupation, avoidance, and dismissiveness; or toward chaos and unpredictability. Our attachment style shapes the way we see others and ourselves, the decisions we make based on these perceptions, and the way they become second nature over time as habitual, unconscious, and automatic conditioned responses of our song-and-dance routines.

As suggested earlier, these patterns act as grafts, or GRAFTS, an acronym for the primary song-and-dance patterns. Keep in mind that while this discussion describes use of these patterns dysfunctionally in the context of irrelationship, the same patterns can be part of healthy adaptive mechanisms as well.

The following examples of adaptive behaviors become grafted onto a child's style of interaction with the world. In adulthood, the grafted behavior continues to be used by the individual to induce a "positive" emotional and behavioral response in others—especially significant others—thus reducing the individual's anxiety.

GRAFTS Descriptors
Good
In the way the child thinks the caregiver wants him or her to be "good." If this technique worked with the caregiver, the individual will try to be "good" in the same way with everyone. The hope is that the good behavior will be "good enough" to fix the caregiver so that he or she can respond to the child in desired ways.

Right

The child is driven to be "right" because he or she thinks that the caregiver will get better and love the child when things are done exactly the way the caregiver wants. Sometimes this can mutate into being "strong" or "competent," both of which are ways of being "right."

Absent

The child believes that, by staying out of the caregiver's way, the caregiver will feel better and will be more able and willing to love the child. This technique is often used by the child of a depressed caregiver who can't be cheered up but also may be deployed by the child of a preoccupied caregiver who seems unwilling to be bothered with the child's problems. Although seemingly counterintuitive at first, this is actually the "beneath-the-radar" strategy employed by the Audience who makes his or her caregiver feel better by listening without bringing up his or her own needs. (Generally, a certain degree of non-engagement, or "absence," is necessary for any of the song-and-dance routines to be successful.)

Funny

The child deliberately assumes the role of entertainer, hoping to make the caregiver laugh. When the child identifies the routine that works, such as acting silly, singing, or dancing, the child redeploys that type of performance anytime the caregiver needs it.

Tense

The child lives in a constant but unconscious state of heightened anxiety. Driven to take care of his or her caregiver, the child constantly "walks on eggshells" but is not allowed to call attention to his or her unease—not even privately. This is a setup for becoming the family scapegoat—the member of the family whom the others identify as "the problem"—thus providing a target for unacknowledged family dysfunction or conflict.

Smart
In families in which intelligence is valued, children become precocious mini-adults so that the caregiver's regard is secured, causing the caregiver to bestow more attention on the child. This behavior often results in the child denying not only his or her feelings but also the freedom to explore areas of interest. As the child matures, he or she uses intellectualization to block the awareness of emotions.

These GRAFTS are some of the techniques we use to gratify our primary caregivers; however, being a compulsive Performer or Audience isn't simply about being good and doing the right thing. Song-and-dance routines can incorporate one or more of the GRAFTS techniques, tailored to the individual's situation, to stabilize his or her environment.

Larry Discovers His GRAFTS

When Larry came into therapy, he couldn't figure out why he was still isolated and alone after a lifetime of trying to impress others and make them like him. Over the course of his therapeutic process, he became familiar with irrelationship, GRAFTS, and song-and-dance routines. One week he brought the following summary of his experience with GRAFTS into session, which he had written in a burst of energetic self-discovery and identification.

My whole life was about GRAFTS. But I never knew I was a people pleaser, a Performer. I just did it automatically with bosses, friends, and everyone.

I was so good at my profession that nobody messed with me. And if I wasn't appreciated in the way I thought I should be, I moved on. I never had trouble finding a new job because I was such a Performer. When I read about GRAFTS, I realized my whole job performance thing goes back to when I was, maybe, two years old.

*I was a **good** boy—always giving the **right** answers to my mom—but I also knew how to be **absent** and stay out of her way!*

Although I was such a Performer, I was uptight and **tense** *the whole time I was being silly or* **funny.** *And, boy was I* **smart!** *Smart enough to game the whole system. I had the entire GRAFTS formula down.*

I was a bank "turnaround" expert: give me a job in a bank that was in trouble and let me work my magic. But one time I played it wrong and was so full of myself that I let them know I found out their game without pointing fingers. Well, they got rid of me all right—what a kick in the butt. My ability to perform literally saved them—some of them from prison—and they thanked me by firing me.

I was drowning in self-pity, but I was determined to fix them, although I was starting to have misgivings. And not just about the dishonesty; I was beginning to see that, no matter how hard I performed, I wasn't getting anything back for it. But I was still thrilled when the president of that company got fired a few years later.

I once saw a plaque on some big-shot's credenza that said "Forgive and Remember." I remember thinking at the time, "That's me!" And before long, I started an investment bank in New York with some Wall Street heavies. We bought a savings and loan in North Carolina that was sinking. In the end, the Fed took away the savings and loan after I caught two of the directors buying shares with insider information. A lot of dirt came out that smeared the company, so I walked away, liquidating whatever interest I had left.

A problem with buying into your GRAFTS is that you make everyone else look like slackers. And I was totally willing—or foolish—enough to walk into every new situation and rub it in, pissing off everybody.

Funny thing is, I did the same thing in my marriage. My wife blamed me for everything that was wrong without any credit for how hard I performed to keep things together. My whole life, personal and professional, was built around impressing other people or trying to make them happy using my GRAFTS. I had no clue that I was just trying to get people to like me.

The other day I heard something on the radio something like, "Don't do what you should do; do what you want to do." It gave me a weird feeling like I had never done that. I somehow realized that I was trapped. I've lived my life trying to please people who couldn't be pleased. In fact, the people I worked hardest at pleasing just sucked up what I put out and then took the money and ran.

Now I can see that this is what my childhood was all about. I desperately used my routines to please my parents, who weren't interested in me. But my routines gave them the perfect out. My parents could tell themselves that I was fine and didn't need them to take care of me. Problem was I wasn't just some professional colleague—I was their kid!

GRAFTS Summary

	Descriptors
G	Good
R	Right
A	Absent
F	Funny
T	Tense
S	Smart

Larry's story shows how deeply GRAFTS become embedded in our behavior, and yet we remain totally unaware of them. We actually become our song-and-dance routines. We create our routines, not because of who we really are, but because we figure out early in life that the people taking care of us respond positively to them. As psychoanalyst and pediatrician Donald Winnicott put it, we unwittingly create a "false self," burying our underdeveloped "true self" deep within us to keep it safe.[2] We persuade ourselves that our caregiver had more interest in the false self than in the fragile true one. This relieves our terror of being left alone in the world with no one to take care of us. But the device works only temporarily, so we repeat the routine the next time we feel unsafe. Before long, we're resorting to it habitually like an addict reaches for a drug. But like that drug, each use of the routine gives us a little less relief. Still, the improvement in the caregiver's behavior is like a fix for both parent and child, thus reinforcing the cycle. We essentially become conditioned by conditional love in place of being liberated by unconditional love. Over time, these mechanisms come to shape how we relate to everyone.

Although varied, the song-and-dance routines share another characteristic: once chosen, they are used uncritically as survival techniques that make the user unable to respond spontaneously and flexibly to life's variables. Instead, the user comes to depend on the same technique as an overall life-management strategy. Winnicott suggests that "the development of a self may involve a sophisticated game of hide and seek in which it is a joy to be hidden but a disaster not to be found." [3] GRAFTS is such a game. In irrelationship terms, an undeveloped or underdeveloped self is deprived of choice and ability to meet life spontaneously. In whatever GRAFTS choice we make, we, like Larry, become locked in a state in which every new situation is a crisis that *must* be managed with our song-and-dance routine. And as you have seen from the stories of Sam and Claire, Glen and Vicky, Hank and Betty, and now Larry, these old habits don't die easily.

Depression and Irrelationship

Irrelationship's anxiety-reducing song-and-dance routines are often accompanied by feelings of despair and hopelessness because of chronically unmet needs and unsuccessful attempts to make things better. The popular application of the term *depression* to almost any negative emotional state has led to a widespread misunderstanding of what clinical depression actually is. Nevertheless, depression is often part of the lives of people affected by irrelationship.

In his well-known essay, "Mourning and Melancholia," Sigmund Freud develops a theory suggesting that depression is related to unconscious mourning. According to the theory, the unconscious is the repository of grief experienced early in life, especially grief resulting from loss of a loved one. This loss produces anger at the lost love object—anger that the self deems unacceptable, leading to inward redirection of the anger, or "introjected rage." This amounts to an attack on the self and denial of the loss by displacing the feelings inward. In the case of Major Depression, the dynamic is devastating; unable to outthink our feelings, we become overwhelmed, even consumed by them, and shut down. However, shut down feelings are not dead. Regardless of our attempts to reject, deny, or reframe our feelings, our actions will finally reveal them.[4]

Although depression defends powerfully against unacceptable feelings, including anxiety,[5] other mechanisms may also come into play to block awareness of feelings, including dissociation, or, in less extreme cases, numbing. Irrelationship is an anxiety-reducing form of dissociation, which, if unchallenged, can block awareness of even desirable emotions. However, as noted previously, lack of awareness does not mean feelings cease to exist or take their toll. In reality, denied feelings continue to be processed in the brain's ventral system in the same way as conscious feelings. But denial increases the likelihood that sooner or later rejected feelings will overwhelm us, resulting in poorly controlled interactions with others about which we may feel embarrassed and ashamed.

This mechanism can be compared to the effects of the medication used by dentists to numb pain. If you inject the medication into the right part of your arm and put your hand in a flame, you won't feel pain, but that won't stop the flame from burning your hand. An added danger is, without the pain alerts from the brain, you won't protect the hand adequately while it's healing from the burn, placing the hand at risk for further harm.

In the same way, being unaware of our feelings leaves us vulnerable to sustaining terrible—even disastrous—pain without knowing anything is wrong and protecting ourselves. This is complicated by our brain's inability to differentiate between acute and chronic pain. We have just as much ability to block awareness of trauma and serious threats as to ignore minor discomfort, without protecting ourselves from the consequences. The protective mechanisms of the brain, although isolated from conscious parts of our brain, will still influence us, but the influence isn't felt or consciously examined.

The compulsive caregiver invested in irrelationship often complains of feeling sad, depressed, or depleted. These feelings may be signals that the song-and-dance routine is wearing thin. Negative feelings he or she has long tried to outthink or ignore are surfacing in unexpected and unrecognizable forms. Anxiety begins to overwhelm the carefully constructed fixer identity and expose deep pain. Like a warning light on an automobile dashboard, this signal can prompt action to determine the source of the unhappy feelings and stop more detrimental things from happening. We may not have learned the vocabulary of emotions as a child, but similar to spoken languages, learning the vocabulary of emotions as an adult, although more difficult, isn't impossible.

The Quick Fix of the Song-and-Dance Routine

Modern medicine and pharmacology have demonstrated that pills can successfully treat infections, diabetes, heart problems, and many other serious health issues. Arguably, we have learned to have similar expectations when it comes to treating emotional problems. The piece that's missing from this approach is the discussion of the price that's paid for not feeling our feelings. Also comparing medical problems and treatments to psychiatric problems and medications is simplistic because psychiatric medications can't target emotional problems as sharply as, for example, antibiotics can address infections.

As noted previously, the label "depression" is often applied to almost any kind of negative emotions, including normal, healthy feelings like sadness. If we habitually use medications to numb our feelings, we jeopardize the process of becoming whole, healthy adults. In this way, the effect of denying emotions can be compared to the effects of habitual heavy drinking, drug use, or gambling.

However, medications can sometimes play an important role in treating serious emotional problems. In addition to managing true clinical depression, antidepressant medications can be helpful in making chronic negative feelings manageable so the patient finds the energy and motivation to address long neglected problems.

Against this background of belief in quick fixes, the song-and-dance routine of people affected by irrelationship becomes more understandable and maybe even more desirable. The Performer and the Audience act as quick fixes for each other's distress in the same way they did for their childhood caregivers. But the idea of eliminating suffering, however seductive, is problematic for the same reasons overuse of medications is problematic; song-and-dance routines become palliative devices that divert attention away from feelings, experiences, and life lessons that are important part of becoming an adult. With our emotional interactions blunted, we lose crucial emotional information about ourselves and other people, causing us to lose the ability to notice and respond authentically to what is going on inside and around us. The possibility of genuine living and loving is gradually but firmly set aside.

Looking again at how the brain works gives us more information on how this can happen. The ability of the child's brain to be shaped and molded, that is, its plasticity ("neuroplasticity"), allows pathways to develop in the brain that later become the venue for the irrelationship pattern. The same plasticity explains why it's easier for a child to learn another language than it is for an adult. (Brain plasticity diminishes over time but doesn't completely disappear and can be stimulated later.) In a concrete way, relationship patterns may be seen as languages that a child will learn automatically if that pattern is part of the milieu in which the child is living.[6] Furthermore, more recent research shows that both the propensity for anxiety as well as the tendency toward certain attachment styles are transmitted from parent to child, generation to generation, through socialization and learning rather than exclusively by biological or genetic influences.[7] The child living in a household dynamic of anxiety and depression will look for ways to palliate this dynamic to improve his or her sense of well-being. When successful, he or she will reapply the technique that worked until some other stimulus compels him or her to change. However, just as learning a new language and the language of emotions are more difficult for adults, learning a new language of relationships is a significant, although by no means an impossible, challenge.

Irrelationship and Trust

"I don't trust her."

"He's lying to me."

"She's going to cheat on me."

"They're going to rob me blind."

"I'm not sure if I can trust myself anymore."

"I used to trust my gut, but now I don't trust my own intuition."

"Why do people I want to help always end up hurting me?"

Most of us have had experiences that prompted us to think or say one or more of the previous statements or questions. But what do we mean by trust?

For most of us trust indicates belief that another person isn't going to lie, cheat, steal from, or otherwise mistreat us. Trust may be based on a first impression or can reflect the feelings developed from many years of living with or around someone. Although our trust may not be based on actual experience, we seem easily to learn to "trust the distrust" we feel for a person or group. We may trust a particular individual for some things and not other things and bitterly complain when someone doesn't live up to our expectations.

We also use the term *trust* to indicate predictability, a knowledge that we know what we are going to get, and we can expect to get it consistently. In some situations, consistent and predictable mediocrity is felt to be more acceptable than hit-or-miss excellence, as in the case of a less expensive restaurant whose product is reasonable and consistent, versus an expensive restaurant that gets mixed reviews.

In a vital sense, then, the song-and-dance routine of irrelationship can and must be trusted since both parties are highly invested in its outcome. Thus the Performer will faithfully maintain a performance while the Audience stays at arm's length while paying, feigning, or refusing attention, depending on the conditions of the routine.

All the same, ripples and rough spots can, and do, break in on irrelationship but are barely tolerated. In behavioral probability statistics, the concept of "regression to the mean" is a technical way of saying that, left to themselves, things will return to close to normal after something unusual occurs. For example, in irrelationship, one or both of the players may register an unusual level of frustration or other feeling, but this is usually so alarming that it's put down quickly with only the slightest recognition that it occurred. Everything rapidly returns to what passes for normal, and the trustworthiness of the irrelationship routine is confirmed.

Another Implication of Trust for Irrelationship

One of the apparent contradictions seen in individuals caught in irrelationship is their high tolerance for certain types of emotional pain, particularly loneliness. This may be related to the blunting of awareness of feelings referred to earlier. In fact, irrelationship is a defense against true connection that drives the individual to fill his or her consciousness and time with taking care of others. The paradox is that this "busy-ness" with others ensures that no profound experience of others—no trust or intimacy—can develop.

The following conversation illustrates a couple stuck in an irrelationship trance. On the surface, the conversation revolves around simple disappointment.

He: You're really not very nice to me.

She: What? Yes, I am. What are you talking about?

He: No, you're not. You just aren't.

She: I am so. You just don't appreciate me.

He: Appreciate you? When you're so hard on me all the time?

She: Hard on you? With all the things I do for you, you think I'm hard on you?

Obviously, each person is dissatisfied with something in the dynamic of the relationship, but neither person is willing to step back and to try to find out what's actually happening. Instead, each is lobbing accusations at the other's unexamined viewpoint without challenging their commitment to irrelationship. Instead they dig in their heels and argue about some undefined idea of "nice." They even forget—dissociate from—happier memories of their shared past, choosing to recall only bad memories and mean things the other has said and done. This allows each person to believe that he or she has proven how "bad" the other person is.

People caught in irrelationship often use this self-protective "I'm right, you're wrong" tactic with spouses, partners, children, friends, and colleagues. By not calling time-out to find out what's actually going on, they recommit to brainlock and remain dissociated. Since it's easier to remember bad things when we're in the same emotional state we were in when they first happened (state-dependent memory), it's also easier to remember bad things when we're in a fight or feeling bad. After a while, all our interactions become fighting and bad memories. And eventually, *all relationships in general* seem bad, prompting us to swear off dating or cultivating other social contacts.

The anxiety that prevents the examination of our own communication makes us even less willing to analyze someone else's communication. Mutual trust—except the unconscious conviction that others are going to follow a dead-end script that leaves us feeling lonely—is nowhere to be seen or heard; although both parties would probably be shocked if accused of such a closed-off perspective. Nevertheless, both are so invested in the idea that the other is wrong that they are perfectly willing to try, convict, and execute the other. A simple questioning of their communication pattern could be enough to open a new door in their relationship, but their investment in the status quo of irrelationship makes such an idea unthinkable.

The low-level hostility often seen in people in brainlock makes them unable to accurately interpret others' communication of vulnerability. Instead, each person is liable to view vulnerability as a negative character trait and will ignore or reject such a signal, providing another opportunity for isolation.

The next story illustrates a combination of the loneliness, lack of trust, disappointment, and communication issues that can arise when two people are deeply invested in their song-and-dance routines.

Sylvia and Tyrone's Irrelationship Stronghold

On the spur of the moment, Sylvia, an overworked 911 dispatcher, decided that she and Tyrone needed a weekend getaway trip to Joshua Tree National Forest in the California desert. Her apparent motivation was a growing sense of estrangement she felt from Tyrone, which she blamed on their busy schedules. She hoped that some time away together would counteract the distance she perceived to be developing between them.

Tyrone worked in an adolescent, substance-abuse treatment facility. He had enrolled in a summer course in family dynamics that required a lot of homework. In addition to his misgivings about spending time away from schoolwork, Tyrone told Sylvia he wasn't thrilled by the idea of vacationing in the desert during the summer. However, he agreed not only because he was reluctant to disappoint Sylvia, but also they both enjoyed making love in out-of-the-way outdoor settings.

After a two-hour drive on a winding, largely deserted road, they reached the park. Up to that point, Tyrone remained reticent concerning his ambivalence about the trip. However, as soon as they entered the park, he uncharacteristically lost control and began complaining about the bad timing of this trip. Reflecting on this sudden outburst later in couples' therapy, Tyrone explained that he felt he had the right to be critical because as the Performer in this relationship, he was the one who did all the work to make things better, which included offering Sylvia his insights on how she might "better herself." In his role as a professional caregiver, Tyrone prided himself on doing the hard work of absorbing the emotional cost of living with someone whose life skills were inferior to his.

For her part, Sylvia skillfully played the part of Audience. She allowed, and even encouraged, Tyrone to talk about what he was learning in his studies and to apply it to her relationships with her friends and sometimes with family members. She also prided herself on having the insight to know when, for the health of their relationship, she and Tyrone needed to take one of their quick vacations. And Tyrone had learned from experience not to cross Sylvia at such times.

During therapy when Tyrone and Sylvia processed what had happened on this particular vacation, Tyrone was unable to recall what made him suddenly express his resentment at being pressed to go away at a particularly bad time for him. But he remembered the conversation that followed, beginning with Sylvia's saying, "All right then—we'll just go home."

Tyrone retorted, "What? Are you some kind of control freak?"

Sylvia lapsed into speechless bewilderment as Tyrone continued, "I've noticed something pretty disturbing about the women in your family. Your grandmother has your grandfather's balls in the palm of her hand. Your mother clipped your father's wings when? On their wedding night? And your sister—no, both your sisters—live with men whose balls they obviously snaked years ago."

This diatribe caught Sylvia off guard, but Tyrone felt proud of his insight and ability to help Sylvia understand her family. When they discussed it later, however, Tyrone saw that his tirade was driven by fear that Sylvia was taking advantage of his Performer role to emasculate him gradually.

When Sylvia didn't reply to Tyrone's criticism of her family, he continued, "My balls are made of steel—they're not yours to play with."

Sylvia stopped the car and said, "If you say one more word, you're out of this car."

"Oh, you're threatening me?"

"Get out."

So Tyrone got out, daring Sylvia, but she drove off, leaving Tyrone stranded in the desert. When Sylvia abandoned her Audience role, Tyrone the Performer was forced to confront how alone he was in his carefully orchestrated irrelationship with Sylvia.

With this confrontation, Tyrone and Sylvia hit bottom, which allowed them to begin breaking out of their song-and-dance routine.

Living by the Script until the Script Shatters

Relationships are more than the sum of their parts, but they are still composed of their parts. A relationship is an amalgam of everything each partner brings into it: genetics, neurobiology, physiologic brain dynamics, family dynamics and history, and, perhaps most significantly, character formation from birth until the present moment. Similarly, character includes the total psychological defenses an individual develops for protection from anxiety related to the difficulties of everyday life. People like Sylvia and Tyrone, seen as pure psychological defenses scraping against each other, are the perfect setup for irrelationship.

A review of Sylvia and Tyrone's story will clarify key points on the road into and out of irrelationship. To evade his anxiety, Tyrone demanded that Sylvia stay in the Audience role to ensure that he appeared generous and helpful. Sylvia reduced the couple's anxiety by seeming to play along. While some role-playing may be pretense, the couple may not be conscious of playing roles even though they may have one eye on the song-and-dance routine while keeping the other eye closed. Brainlock demands that both parties stick to the script, although Sylvia's deviation opened the door to their becoming aware that they were trapped in irrelationship. Exhausted and hitting bottom together, they accepted that their script disallowed freedom and spontaneity in their life together. This was the beginning of recovery and building a loving and reciprocal relationship.

Priming Our Roles

Another powerful way to maintain the emotional distance in irrelationship—avoiding intimacy, empathy, emotional risk, and investment—is to trigger, consciously or not, familiar, ingrained roles and play them out together. As we will see with Allison and Justin, we can actually prime our interactions so that they call up defenses that protect us from getting too close.

Allison: I have something I want to talk about, which happened the other night, but I'm scared to say anything because you'll just attack me.

It's the same way I felt with my father. He never wanted to listen. He didn't seem like he wanted to be bothered. He would sort of listen, then interrupt and take over the conversation, telling me what he thought. Well, you're just like him. He didn't have any patience. But it wasn't what he said; he just looked at me like I was a total piece of garbage.

Justin: Well, give me a minute to think of things I would say in order to retaliate appropriately.

Allison: Even *that word* makes me feel on edge.

Justin: Appropriately? What's wrong with *that word*?

Allison: No, retaliate. It makes me anxious; you always say stuff like that.

Justin: Actually, I was just kidding. You seem so worried about how I'm going to react, so sure I am going to say mean things. It almost makes me feel obligated to respond the way you expect. It's like I'm being set up to act like a jerk because it's what you want deep down. And it makes me nervous too because before I say a word, I feel you've decided I'm going to be mean like your father. Before we even start I'm getting defensive because it's easier than actually communicating. And then I get screwed over anyway. So why even bother?

Role suction is a term used to describe how people get pulled into familiar relationship roles from their past.[8] Although two people—a speaker and a listener—think they are in new situations, the speaker is actually recreating situations from childhood that evoke his or her negative self-perceptions. A *negative empathy* develops in which the listener hears and responds to the speaker and unconsciously replies with the response the speaker is afraid the listener will have. Negative views of self surface in the listener, and he or she ends up feeling that trying to have a different conversation is useless. Anticipating attack, the listener takes protective measures against what he or she thinks the speaker is going to say, searching his or her memory for what went wrong earlier in the week and—expecting to get attacked for it—devises counterattacks. This approach sets up the listener to react in the way the speaker originally said he or she wanted to prevent. Both are left unhappy and unable to understand why it went wrong again when they were both trying hard to make it different this time.

Toward Positive Change

1. Reflect on stressful experiences from your childhood. What unspoken agreements did you make with parents or others in your family so things would be okay in your household? What was going on that made the agreement necessary? What did the unspoken agreement change in yourself and in your family?

2. Reflect on a relationship in your life that you believe was, or is, affected by irrelationship. It can be with a family member, friend, romantic interest, or someone in your workplace. What was, or is, wrong with that relationship? What would you change about it if you could? How would you begin the process of changing it? (Don't be afraid to say, "I don't know.")

3. Which of the GRAFTS patterns is familiar to you? Whom did you use GRAFTS with and how?

Pathways to Empathy

- Think of a difficult time in your life in which someone reached out and gave you space for your feelings. How did that person do that, and what did it do for you?

- Experiences of this type are essential to our humanity. How could you pass along a similar experience to another person?

Part Two

Getting to Know You

Spotlight on the Performer and the Audience

Chapter 5

The Performer—Intuition Backfires into Isolation

You're always being told how amazing you are. You always seem to know what people are feeling even before they do. You have a reputation for being sensitive, caring, and generous. And it isn't surprising people say these things about you because you're constantly looking to do things for your partner. You seem to have a sixth sense that tips you off about what someone wants or needs even before he or she does. You answer questions in a way that seems so responsive and makes the person laugh while you carefully guard against saying anything that might be taken the wrong way. Yes, it's exhausting, almost a full-time job, but you are proud of telling others, "All I want to do is make you happy." It seems to make you feel needed and loved.

Is the Performer really that good at knowing what others think and feel? Or does the Performer just have an inkling about others' unmet needs and fills in the blanks without bothering to look into the feelings that may be attached? Maybe for the Performer, this uncanny and even seductive ability to guess others' needs is more like a game than anything else. Or perhaps, some hidden part of the Audience is watching from the wings, feeding the right lines to say.

Carol and Kate's Irrelationship Storyline

Snuggled up on the couch after spending much of the evening enjoying (at least ostensibly) an elaborate meal, Carol became aware of an unfamiliar lack of gratitude from her wife, Kate. Suddenly Carol had a sense that something was seriously wrong. From the beginning of their relationship, she had possessed an intuitive sense of exactly how to please Kate, specifically related to all things culinary—or so Carol had come to believe.

"Kate . . . " Carol begins, "Honey? Is everything . . . "

But before Carol could continue, Kate—perhaps for the first time ever—stands up, stomps her feet, and explodes, "I've had enough."

What could be wrong?

The basis of what Carol and Kate believed to be intimacy between them revolved around food, which grew out of messages both had received early in life that connected love with food. Although each internalized the message differently, Carol fueled their shared interest because she believed she had the extraordinary ability to gauge Kate's desire for a particular meal and prepare it for her. However, her efforts and Kate's reception of them did not invariably lead to a satisfactory outcome for either of them.

Kate was an only child and felt that her parents stuffed her with whatever they could—mostly food—to make up for their ineptitude at providing Kate with the essentials necessary for childhood development, particularly social skills. She described her parents as extremely anxious and affected by a vague fear that harm would come to their daughter if she were not given proper nutrients. Thus providing food and nutrients became a stand-in for actual nurturing behavior. Kate later came to see this unending stream of food as compensation for growing up lonely and sad. For their part, Kate's parents had an insatiable need for recognition and approval from their daughter.

In contrast, Carol was the only girl and the youngest child among four siblings. For Carol, the "food is love" message led her, while still very young, to cultivate cooking skills and use them to claim acceptance and importance in her competitive family. Her cooking also helped to reduce the anxiety of her financially strapped mother and father. However, Carol's expertise in the kitchen became a means of exercising control by feeding others while denying meals to herself.

For Kate, Carol's insistence on feeding her was stifling in the same way that her parents' pressing food on her was stifling. She finally permitted the breakthrough that allowed her to see how their shared song-and-dance routine was harming both of them. The seamless transition Kate and Carol had made together from their dysfunctional childhood roles abruptly hit a wall. Kate's unexpected rejection of Carol's caretaking saved their marriage.

Intuition and the Brain

The practice of *intuition* varies widely from person to person. But brain science tells us a lot about how this extrasensory perception develops. Intuition is vital to the success of the Performer. As a right-brain (nonverbal) ability, intuition begins to develop early in life—years before the ability to talk develops any sophistication of intent or process. This is because the infant is born with a more developed right-brain hemisphere and needs to relate nonverbally with caregivers immediately. The infant is born with predispositions toward other people, a tilt toward certain attachment styles and away from others and greater or lesser tendency for resilience. Greater resilience is associated with more secure attachment style and with a greater ability to deal effectively with poor caregiving. For example, a more resilient child is more likely to seek a surrogate caregiver who provides better care than his own parent rather than passively becoming caught up in his parent's irrelationship-generating approach.

The left brain, which is the site of formulated thinking and analytic reasoning, develops about eighteen months later than the right brain. An implication of this is that before we can deliberately use memory, our brain has already begun laying down patterns about everything, including relationships. Before the individual is verbal, patterns related to irrelationship are already in place. When such early patterns are threatened, rigid protective mechanisms are deployed to maintain the individual's safety.

Over time this rigidity becomes an unrecognized habit—an overlay affecting relationships with parents, siblings, and everyone else. For the child—and, later, the adult—this overlay is a key survival adaptation that, absent any intervention, will continue indefinitely.

As the individual enters adolescence, he or she unconsciously but vigilantly applies protective skills to prevent injury. In adulthood, this same individual becomes the parent who requires his or her needs to be met silently without drawing attention. But the rigidity is passed to the child, who is forced to develop a sixth sense for detecting others' needs—in fact, it becomes second-nature. Without knowing it, the individual deflects circumstances that had previously threatened the equilibrium with his or her parents, prompting emotional outbursts and erratic behavior that were frightening as a child. At first the cues are unnoticeable to anyone not invested in the situation and may be as varied as speed of gait, quality of voice (or silences), or the manner of closing doors. Painful experience has taught the child to heed these signals and deploy the necessary measures to circumvent an unpleasant scene.

In adolescence and adulthood, this individual may figure out that picking a preemptive fight may head off a more disturbing encounter. Rather than getting caught off guard, striking first allows time for mental preparation and actually sets off a more predictable encounter. Here again, brain science offers how these techniques become etched into the functioning of our brains.

The *mirror neuron system* was originally discovered by accident. Researchers noticed that in nonhuman primates, a group of neurons mirrored the animals' observable physical gestures. Closer investigation revealed that mirror neurons were found in every part of the motor system, that is, the areas of the brain that make parts of the body move. The nervous system was found to include a platform for remembering and unconsciously integrating triggers, cues, and markers of the emotional state and intentions of others—especially the crucial people in our lives—helping to get the information necessary to drive intuition and provide a foundation for empathy by using the basic information from mirror neurons to make unconscious decisions about other people's inner states from their actions.

In addition to this, certain other specialized cells known as *spindle neurons* create links among other groups of cells throughout the brain, thus constructing an information-sharing network that supports the function of intuition. Still other neurons, named *oscillators*, help coordinate movements between people, unconsciously choreographing the subtle dance that is always going on. The value of this mechanism is obvious; it provides actionable information to the individual's consciousness that allows him or her to head off negative experiences with others if evasive maneuvers have been ineffective.[1]

Most people raised in stressful situations during childhood emerge with highly developed intuitive skills. They also typically bring strong biases, distortions, and misperceptions of motives to encounters with others that detrimentally—even fatally—condition how they see relationships. A common example of this is that they often make errors in both directions when deciding whom to trust and not to trust. Such people have no idea how distorted their interpretation of others is. They're totally unconscious of their filtering mechanisms and often are irrationally convinced their interpretation is the only correct view of things. This is a recipe for disaster if there ever was one—having totally convinced yourself of a distorted view of the world for which you will fight to the death to preserve.

As intimated earlier, the true feelings of each partner involved in irrelationship is actually irrelevant to the other. What is important is that each partner adheres to their song-and-dance routine without deviating from the carefully choreographed steps designed to make each other feel better. Of course, false steps may disturb the performance at first—particularly in cases where a partner's intuition isn't well honed. This may cause pain to the other partner at first, but an attentive response and willingness to adapt will go a long way to reducing the impact of initial errors.

The Performer's need—the demand—to be in control has an ironic, unrecognized impact on the Audience. It results in a devaluing of any personal traits or contributions the Audience may be able to make to their shared relationship, as we saw with Kate's response to Carol's "food is love" routine. Kate's role and usefulness as the Audience is confined to showing appreciation to the Performer. Similarly, the Audience requires that the Performer, Carol in this case, confine herself to saying and doing only things that make Kate feel better. In this position of superiority and power, Carol is not allowed to reveal any need or vulnerability. So while the Performer role appears to set the agenda and determine the dynamic parameters, in reality, the Audience implicitly places comparably rigorous demands on the Performer in the "straitjacket built for two."

Both roles are tools for managing or preventing awareness of pain. The emotional numbness that sets in over time increasingly renders the Performer unprepared to recognize the approach of danger and unable to properly interpret signals that his or her intuition formerly recognized as signs of emotional disturbance in both partners. Having lost this capacity, the Performer cannot effectively communicate the need for change, let alone make choices to bring about change, and can't call for renegotiation of the song-and-dance routine. Instead, she either turns off the pain or creates the self-aggrandizing but masochistic pleasure of submitting to it. But generally, the Performer believes that he or she wants nothing more than to be helpful and appreciated by partners who really need his or her help. However, as noted earlier, since you can't outthink your feelings, becoming able again to feel pain is part of the setup for blowing irrelationship apart.

Although the Performer's song-and-dance routine seems to work for a time, the following stories illustrate why the modulated interaction between partners is hollow and does nothing to lessen the pain it was designed ironically to relieve. Sadly it usually ends in more anxiety for both parties.

George the Performer Gives, Gives, and Gives

George, a middle-aged man and self-described tough guy, was beginning to break through the bravado he had contrived to cover his feelings. He was finally able to discuss with his therapist what it had been like—what it felt like—to have gone to prison as a young man for a series of crimes related to substance abuse. As he clutched his stomach, tears began to roll down his face for the first time in many years. Finally he managed to say, "What a relief to finally tell my story."

Before he became a tough guy, George had always been a good guy. He was a perfect example of a Performer. George was the oldest child of a family with a severely depressed mother and a raging alcoholic father. As far back as he could remember, George had taken it upon himself to take care of his mother and two younger brothers. Although he gave generously, he felt that no one appreciated what he had to offer. Reflecting back many years later, George admitted that he also felt that no one had anything of value to offer him. He became accustomed to severe deprivation and took pride in being able to withstand it, which, to him, was the definition of strength. It never occurred to him to wonder whether or not he would have been open to receiving anything anyone could give. Finally, he did come to the realization that being the good guy wasn't doing anything for him and was probably harming him. He felt sickeningly frustrated that, although the caregiving that he gave to his family was necessary for their survival (including his father's), doing so didn't seem to improve his standing in the family or win any affection. "No one appreciated anything I did for them—no one at all," he stated. Nevertheless, he stuck to his role of family savior.

People locked in situations like this without getting any recognition or validation often look for ways to reward themselves. The problem is the satisfaction of patting oneself on the back doesn't go deep or last long. It can be compared to substituting masturbation or casual sex for intimacy with a valued partner or spouse; after the experience, the individual is still isolated and scanning the environment for the next encounter, hoping it will somehow prove to be more satisfying than the last time. Meanwhile, the tough-guy routine makes it harder to see one's own vulnerability, and the constant state of hypervigilance gets in the way as it does for a soldier who behaves as if he's still in the battle zone after he returns home. Letting the troubled feelings lead the tough guy to decide that something is wrong is a giant step beyond simply feeling pain.

One day in therapy, as his birthday approached, George revealed for the first time to anyone that when he was a child he always got a bad pain in his gut when his birthday approached—sometimes so bad he had to go to the emergency room. When this happened, his whole family would come to the hospital—the only time they showed up for him—bringing a party to his bedside in the emergency room. And this included not only his immediate but also his extended family. Of course, it never crossed his mind that his annual attack of abdominal pain was a device George used unconsciously to manipulate his family into showing him some attention and care.

Recalling this was humiliating for George. And as he looked at his own family life, he could see that he had passed the same pattern on to his son. His son had been the good guy in the family who protected his mother and two sisters from George's alcohol-fueled rage and violence. And George despised him for it—despised him for being the kind of Performer that George had been in the face of *his* father's rage. George became afraid his son would also end up isolated and unable to feel good about taking care of the family. Although George understood that he had turned his son into himself, his son's abandonment of the family left George resentful and deeply angry.

After remaining abstinent from alcohol and drugs for ten years, George began to recognize how his untreated trauma had harmed his life and his children's lives. He was particularly shaken to realize that his son had left home at the same age that he, George, went to prison the first time. He was unable to deny the shock of recognition he felt when his son shouted, "You take care of them," as he left home, leaving behind his mother and sisters.

The stories discussed up to this point primarily represent profiles in which the participants in irrelationship were led as children to believe that the song-and-dance routines they administered to their caregivers succeeded in making their caregivers feel better. They carried this delusion through life offering (or imposing) their caretaking on others. However, if the treatment offered didn't fix the caregiver, or, as in George's case, if the dysfunction in the family was too disturbed to respond to the child's treatment, the child will be deprived of safety and security, resulting in trauma he or she will try to repair in future connections with others. In either case, the child clings to the Performer-caretaker role in future interactions.

As can be seen, the Performer's song-and-dance routine—do-gooder, rescuer, and even hero—are blatant cover-ups for anxiety. In the context of irrelationship, the Performer's compulsive song-and-dance routine typically developed along one of these lines:

- Attempts to change the caregiver.
- Attempts to change him- or herself to please the caregiver.
- Allows the caregiver to get away with poor caregiving by avoiding the caregiver. Underlying this, the child assumes that the caregiver's avoidance is somehow his or her fault and responds by insulating him- or herself.
- Ignores deep, unpleasant feelings or profound, negative experiences to avoid bringing personal anxiety into the open.
- Acclimates to feelings of deprivation by interpreting them as proof of how good he or she is.

Gloria the Performer Faces the Truth

At seventy years old, Gloria presented herself as a force of nature. Her energy and youthfulness, she claimed, was "God-given," without cosmetic enhancement or surgery. She developed and sustained a complicated and well-versed professional song-and-dance routine for singles' dances and had done so through most of her adult life. In fact, her earliest memory was of performing for the entire sleep-away summer camp that her parents sent her and her brother to when she was four years old.

Something about this casually delivered piece of information struck her therapist as odd. "Four seems awfully young to be sent away for the summer."

She responded, "Before we left for camp that summer, my brother and I had been told our mother had to go away, and the camp was making a special exception. When we returned from camp, my mother *and* my father were gone. My aunt had taken over the childcare for my brother and me.

She told us to tell everyone she was our mother now—our real mother was dead, and we would not be seeing our father again."

Gloria and her brother spent the next two years adjusting to the idea that they would never see their parents again. However, on some level Gloria wasn't buying it. "I felt it in my gut that I could bring Mom back." She prayed hard for two years, promising God that if her mother returned to her she would be good for the rest of her life and would take care of her mother forever. Gloria later found out that the story about her mother's supposed death was not entirely a lie. Moreover, she remembered the voices of doctors, her aunt, and even her mother and father, saying her mother was very sick with tuberculosis, needed to go to a sanitarium, and was not expected to live. Years later, she discovered another part of the truth she had long suspected. After her mother went to the sanitarium, her father ran off with another woman. However, the story she was told was obviously—even to her at the time—full of deceptions, partial truths, and out-and-out lies.

Nevertheless, skeptical as she had been, Gloria was shocked when, without any preparation, her mother and father simply returned without any explanation. Her prayers, it seemed, had been answered. What miraculous power this little girl must have believed she had that she was able—through her hopes, dreams, and prayers—to put back together her shattered world by bringing her mother back to life. Again, earliest relationship patterns are imprinted on the brain even before a child can fully make sense of the world through language. This helps explain how Gloria processed these events. In this case, the upshot was that the early experience of the supposed death and return of her mother left Gloria, almost seven decades later, with a four-year-old's fragile, incomplete ability to process death and loss.

Years later, when Gloria had perfected her song-and-dance routine, she proved repeatedly that she knew how to find lost souls needing someone to "bring them back from the dead." She became a Performer who performed miracles. When she first came into therapy, Gloria's presenting problem was that she had been involved with a bipolar man twenty years her junior whose mood swings ranged from suicidal depression to homicidal rage. By the time she decided she needed therapy, she had lived in this situation for nine-and-a-half years. However, real problems developed when her partner went into therapy and was told by his therapist that if he wanted to get better he'd have to end his relationship with Gloria.

"Imagine that," she quipped sarcastically at the end of session one day. "After all I've done for him."

The history behind the irrelationship is that Gloria saw him and plucked him from a loveless marriage, although he remained legally married. He had acted just as her father had when her mother was hospitalized—flying the coop when things got difficult. Gloria then proceeded to create a love nest for the two of them in the lower east side of Manhattan. When her partner's depression and mood instability didn't improve, Gloria expanded her song-and-dance routine by including him in her professional work as an entertainer. However, by ignoring his less-than-stellar abilities as a singer and his destructive drinking, they got themselves sidelined from performing in highly regarded venues in which Gloria had been previously sought after. She began to refer to her partner sarcastically as "Billy Sinatra" and began to become resentful, feeling that he had "shaken me down for the best of my goods."

Meanwhile, Billy Sinatra's mood swings began to improve when he finally began to take his medication as ordered. This was countered by an increase in Gloria's anxiety level. For years she had believed that her generosity had saved Billy Sinatra's life, but his positive response to his medication unhinged her elaborately contrived understanding of the success of their personal and professional life together.

As his mood disorder resolved, Billy Sinatra began to feel that he was the one who had been "shaken down." He audaciously suggested that leaving his wife and contributing to their living expenses were his worthwhile contributions to their shared life. Even more galling, he had come to see himself as a meaningfully contributing partner to their theater work. Gloria dismissed this out-of-hand claim, "Ha. Not–at–all. Billy Sinatra has extorted and exploited the very best that I have to offer—and now he's threatening to leave me, alone and empty." Gloria insisted she was the only one who had what it took to make it. And to make matters worse, now, after exploiting her for so long, Billy Sinatra was talking about taking up with a younger woman as men had done all her life.

Gloria's story illustrates the all-but-certain outcome of functioning as a Performer in irrelationship. In the years since she first started taking care of her caregivers, Gloria did the same thing with virtually everyone she encountered. The result was that she was chronically drained by those around her, all the while denying them any value of significance of their own, apart from what she was able to do for them. This repeatedly drove others away, including potential love matches. The threat of once again being left alone forced Performer Gloria to take a look at the history of isolation and resentment that always seemed to ensue when left alone with herself. After long-term therapy, she began to realize that her song-and-dance routine hadn't been all that good for her audiences. A major corner was turned when she began to refer to her loyal theater following as "The Walking Wounded."

The Performer's Belief in Omnipotence

The child who thinks actions—song-and-dance routines—solved his or her parent's problems develops a misleading sense of power—even omnipotence. However, without knowing why the actions worked, the child lacks the information needed to understand what happens between him- or herself and others. Believing that one can make his or her parents happy or fix their problems leads to faulty self-assumptions—that one is talented, smart, important, and amusing—perhaps even grown-up. Such a child is rewarded for the wrong kinds of things (taking too much care of others, being a cheerleader, or taking responsibility immediately and inappropriately for fixing problems) rather than for the right kinds of things (showing awareness of others' needs in balance with one's own needs, learning boundaries, frustration tolerance, or response inhibition). Such a child is, among other things, poorly prepared to learn from failure. Thus, the child's self-image and style of relating with others is shaped to fit the confused environment in which he or she is raised, leading to misguided conclusions about reality, especially social reality.

Drawing such conclusions arises from the desperate need to feel that one can ensure his or her own safety. From there the child comes to believe that using his or her special ability will fix the parent or caregiver whenever necessary. Belief in this special ability will have a crucial impact on the development of the child's personality. The child will exercise this ability not only on caregivers but everyone around him or her to keep them happy—at least, the highly self-selected group of people who will stick around with someone who acts that way.

Judy the Performer: When It's Not So Smart to be Smart

At five years old, Judy was an endless source of delight and entertainment for her strict academician father. She knew the answers to all of his questions and was driven to impress all of her grammar school peers with her quick wit and intelligence. Her smart song-and-dance routine (the S in GRAFTS) continued as Judy moved through high school and college. In her professional life, she obsessively was compelled to impress not only her colleagues but also her husband and children with her smarts.

Problems arose when Judy was unable to free herself from the need to prove herself to others. She always had to be the one with the right answers. And in the process, she lost the ability to learn from others and couldn't recognize her own mistakes. It was exhausting for Judy and impacted negatively on relations with friends, peers, and family. When Judy went to the university and began her professional life, those around her, including her superiors, had no difficultly recognizing her intelligence, but her constant need to one-up them became tedious and tiresome. In a workplace where competence is expected of everyone, Judy's demand for recognition became annoying to her coworkers and detracted from their ability to function as a team.

Judy also began to lose the appreciation of her family. When her treatment of her family crossed the line into controlling, manipulative, and even demeaning behavior, they complained of feeling violated and abused.

People with extreme cases of needing to manipulate and manage others are often considered toxic, highlighting the ambiguous but powerful influence the irrelationship dynamic has on others not directly involved. Its effects can make the difference between who gets a job, a promotion, or a second date. Over time it alienates that person's entire group of friends and associates. This irrelationship dynamic, based on a childhood survival routine to please a father can end up filtering out the possibility of important and meaningful real relationships without Judy, in this case, ever knowing it's happening.

The Performer Who Needs His Audience to Stay Stuck

The Performer often finds the routine for managing interpersonal relationships doesn't work as well as he or she thinks it should no matter how much effort is invested. In fact, the Performer sometimes gets the feeling he or she is actually pushing away people without understanding why.

Harry, an extreme Performer, was driven by a compulsion to take care of those around him. He was finally all but forced into therapy by the negative reactions and resentment his caring seemed to create. His story is a good example of how irrelationship works like an addiction; it provides relief—even a kind of euphoria—but also creates a need for more of the same. And, as in the case of a substance addiction, as tolerance builds, the caretaking becomes increasingly frenzied to achieve the needed level of relief. This mechanism has a physiological basis in which the "chemical reward" in the brain generated by the excitement of a new relationship is never quite as good as it was early in the relationship. Some of the luster and excitement of first love is lost, but the memory of the initial high can keep us coming back for more in hopes of repeating it. Sometimes this results in self-destructive behavior. Severe childhood distress can, in some people, result in a variation in the way pain is processed by the body, causing them to experience pleasure even from self-mutilation. In such persons, the appropriate warning systems have been impaired or shut down, strengthening the barrier between Performer and other people and contributing to an unconscious perception that other people are objects to be controlled and even owned.

Now, back to Harry. Harry treated his anxiety by trying to fix the woman he married. "Give, give, give, until it hurts," could be his motto. A forty-five-year-old engineer, Harry came for treatment when his marriage reached a crisis. He worried that his wife, also an engineer who he met on the job, seemed to become increasingly indifferent, emotionless, and compliant in their relationship, deferring to him in everything.

Harry felt that he knew enough to connect his wife's moods and behavior to her upbringing that she described as painful. And for a Performer like Harry, this was enough of a cue for his song-and-dance routines. They were elaborate, including the GRAFTS behaviors of being good, right, and smart. When his treatment seemed to improve her moods, he became elated, feeling that his success made his own life worthwhile. His professional success and his wife's regard for him fed his incentive to devote time and energy to treating his wife's moods.

Things took a bad turn when Harry, passed over for a promotion at work, accused his new female supervisor of discrimination. In the ensuing power struggle, he lost his job. Nothing like this had ever happened to Harry; he was accustomed to success, being liked by everyone around him, and regarding himself as practically invincible. Losing his job was a blow to Harry's ego and his sense of security.

As his life unraveled, Harry turned to his wife, who, to his dismay, was unprepared to take care of him and unable to express feelings for his situation that one may expect in a committed life-partner. She had always relied on him for support and had been a good Audience, but her investment in their relationship did not include a willingness to reverse roles in the event that he needed her active support. In fact, she was unable to convey that she grasped the crisis created by his job loss. She offered only her increasingly typical blank stare that masked her own repressed emotional state. She certainly had no song-and-dance routine in the ready to make Harry feel better. She had never played the Performer and was locked into her Audience role with great numbing skill.

Realizing that he was basically facing this life-crisis in isolation, Harry became furious, feeling that he had been used, betrayed, and abandoned. For his wife's part, Harry's anger prompted her to allow herself, for the first time, to realize that Harry looked down on her and saw her as damaged and inferior.

In his therapeutic process, Harry discovered that he had cheered up all the significant women in his life, beginning at five years old—the year his mother developed a medical condition that often left her physically depleted and unable to be present for her child. Her decreased presence and emotional state so frightened Harry that he became her caregiver, going so far as preparing her meals and sleeping in the same bed with her. Being her little man made Harry feel safe, important, and even like a grown-up. The role distortion continued until Harry left home for graduate school. Meanwhile it complicated his maturation process, including developmental tasks such as establishing age-appropriate relationships with peers, elders, and authority figures. The effects of these uncompleted tasks dogged Harry both in the workplace and in his attempts at intimate relationships. Over time, Harry realized that he hadn't selected a wife who he could regard as a peer or was prepared to be his partner; he had selected someone who would soak up his relentless caregiving.

As the deterioration of their relationship became apparent, Harry grew mystified by his wife's cold compliance with anything he said or wanted to do. However, the place they took in one another's lives mirrored the relationship he acted out with his mother. His wife expected him to stay in the starring role of Performer and withdrew from him the moment imperfections in that façade appeared. But even when this insight occurred, Harry was a long way from understanding that he and his wife both demanded and resented the roles they were playing for the other. The fact that Harry needed his wife to be his Audience was jarring—just as jarring as realizing they had created a scenario which could only leave them feeling resentful that they were not meeting each other's needs.

Harry was shell-shocked; however, he was able to be in touch with his hurt and fear just enough for him to be able—and willing—to feel this as a window of opportunity. In that moment, he was able to re-examine his history of isolation and see his part in it. He realized throughout their marriage, except when he was under the utmost duress, he forbade (through actions more so than words) his wife from contributing to him at all. He saw that his sudden desperation was a setup that assured his wife's failure.

Through that insight, Harry was willing to let go of the reins and invite his wife to join him in restarting their relationship. This invitation was, at first reluctantly, accepted and was parlayed into a process of exploring their difficulties together. Rather than seeing and treating their relationship and each other as a problem to be solved, they began to create a process whereby they could both assess their problems as well as their assets (both individual and joint). They eventually used this newfound information to create a partnership and were shocked to discover they had become allies.

In this chapter, we've seen examples of extreme Performers. Their apparent generosity reveals a need to maintain distance from emotions related to love and caring. In Parts 4 and 5 of this book, we will discover ways to defuse these frenzied patterns and find a way out of the irrelationship trap.

Toward Positive Change

1. **Do you find yourself expected, implicitly or explicitly, to do for others because no one else will? What things do you do?**

2. **Do you feel that others expect you to pick up the slack at home or at work? Give examples and discuss how it makes you feel.**

3. After doing things for others, are you sometimes left feeling unsatisfied or even resentful? Give examples.

4. When your partner is unhappy, does it make you worry that things might be falling apart? How does this affect you? Why?

5. Do you have difficulty asking for help? Do you know why? Elaborate and cite examples of good and bad outcomes when you have asked someone to help you with a task or a personal problem.

6. Do your romantic relationships often seem to start up quickly and then fall apart in more or less the same way? Give examples of what caused them to end.

Chapter 6

The Audience—Resisting Care

You cannot believe your luck. You've fallen in love. And this time, you know this is the one. And he or she is crazy about you and takes care of your every need even before you're aware of it. You feel hopeful and alive. You're waited on hand and foot, and your new partner always comes across as smart, helpful, and funny. At last you've met the person who's going to make your life right. With this partner, you will never be lonely, and he or she will be able to depend on you always to give the love and support he or she wants and needs—forever.

If this sounds familiar, you are mainlining irrelationship straight into your blood and brain. This shot is a cocktail of brain chemistry that includes dopamine, vasopressin, glutamate, oxytocin, testosterone, and other hormones—or, in less technical terms, a hit of pure pleasure and safety.

As the Audience you might also feel the Performer is draining you or a lot of your conversations revolve around diagnosing and fixing your shortcomings. Sometimes the Performer seems almost harshly critical, but usually you feel grateful and relieved to have someone in your life who is so concerned about your welfare. What's wrong with this perfect partnership? What's wrong with making nice all of the time? Almost inevitably, the relationship backfires, and things begin to disintegrate. Why, if it's so wonderful, does that happen?

In spite of how great it might look from the outside, after a time, things don't feel right to both partners. Your Performer partner starts to feel underappreciated. Things start to feel two dimensional, or flat like a cardboard cutout, rather than truly alive. Your partner is often silently resentful. You begin to feel like a captive Audience, living on a one-way street that isn't going your way. Feeling frozen and unable to effectively fight or flee, your brain's fear system is getting burned out. You're reaching your tipping point because things aren't the same anymore. You need a break. Something needs to change—and fast. One day you get the nerve to say you aren't getting what you want, even though things look so good. You have tried to express the feelings and needs that have been building inside you, but they have been ignored. So now you're feeling that you no longer want them ignored.

What has changed is that your need to enjoy the Performer's routine is becoming outweighed by an increasing need for autonomy and individuality. You find yourself worried and cringing inwardly at your partner's performances. Unable any longer to validate your partner, you start to pull away, wondering if the whole thing has been an illusion or a mistake. When did you give up all your power—your right to have a say in the relationship? You wonder, *Have I been seduced? Betrayed? Who is this person who has been controlling everything?* You could not possibly guess that your whole manner of relating to others was designed to invite and sustain this pattern. This is your song-and-dance routine to keep you safe from the threat of your feelings, emotions, and past unmet needs.

You—the Audience—begin to push denial aside and look at the reality of the relationship. The Performer begins to look like a control freak. You begin to wonder if something besides generosity and love is what motivates all the performing, so you feel betrayed, vacillating between anger at the Performer and yourself. Sometimes confusion and disgust at oneself manifests physically as nausea or dizziness, and you may feel a sense of loss and sadness.

Like the Performer, the Audience suffers as a result of the commitment to a defense system calculated to keep him or her isolated and alone, but the Audience exhibits this commitment in an insatiable need to connect with someone who will cure, fix, or save him or her. When the two find one another, they devise an impenetrable barrier to an authentic shared life. They co-create and sustain a state of safe disconnection designed to exclude spontaneous interaction with the world they cannot control. In this insular irrelationship system, the Audience is able to check out. If, perchance, the Audience finds that the Performer's self-devised song-and-dance routine fails to address his or her needs, the Audience will prompt the Performer to alter the routine. When both parties consent to this ongoing arrangement, the result is a jointly devised maze—a framework for their life—from which exit seems undesirable, yet they desire to exit so they can live an authentic life.

Mai the Extreme Audience

"I screamed and yelled. For no reason, I came running up behind him while he was changing our daughter's diapers and hit him. I told him I was going to call the police. I pulled the baby out of his arms and threatened him. But he had done nothing. He had done nothing."

For Mai, this scene was surprising. Her song-and-dance routine was disappearing, certainly not engaging in messy emotional entanglements. Although she did not know it then, she was approaching rock bottom and could no longer perform her routine, feeling isolated and desperate. With this window of opportunity, Mai and her husband, Glen, had the chance to revive their love.

Mai always sat quietly and unobtrusively in the back seat and, when necessary, vanished entirely. She had made marginalizing herself an art form, particularly in intimate relationships. She let others perform while she quietly fantasized about her escape. But on this occasion, she unaccountably blew up at her husband.

Mai was born in a rural village near the coast of the Sea of Japan to parents whose marriage had been arranged. Mai had been born with a congenital deformity that, at the time, typically resulted in premature death. However, at the point at which her parents abandoned hope for Mai's survival, a Tokyo surgeon agreed to come to their village to perform an innovative surgical procedure, which gave Mai a normal life expectancy.

In most families this tragedy-turned-miracle would have been regarded as an occasion for rejoicing. However, Mai's paternal grandmother regarded the birth as ill-omened and shameful. She humiliated Mai's mother for bringing defective offspring into the family and continued to do so until her death when Mai was twelve years old.

Like many Japanese of that time, Mai's grandmother, father, and her father's two siblings emerged from World War II severely traumatized and starving. Against this background and the grandmother's traditional, fatalistic worldview, an unsatisfactory child's birth was seen as a curse to be blamed on Mai's mother. Mental health professionals refer to this family loading as intergenerational or transgenerational transmission of trauma.

Although never clinically diagnosed, Mai's mother was severely depressed throughout this period. Mai's response to her mother's emotional state was simply to watch her mother's performance as a martyr. Whenever possible, she disappeared in order to avoid adding to the burden and tragedy of her mother's life. A quiet child who asked for nothing, she received what she asked for. She even took pains to occupy as little space in their home as possible and, in imitation of her mother, scarcely ate.

Mai was fairly successful at distancing herself from her family's joyless household. She reasoned that little was to be gained by her quietly attending to her mother's pain. But Mai sensed that something else was off—something had happened in their family history that involved her more actively than she realized. Unfortunately she had no inkling of what it was or of how to find out about it.

When she was eighteen years old, Mai's intuition was confirmed; her mother told Mai about how she had cursed the gods for her life and marriage, her flawed child, and the continual abuse she believed herself obligated to accept from her mother-in-law. When her mother revealed this story, Mai exploded at her mother (as she exploded at her husband at the beginning of this section). Soon afterward, Mai left home for Tokyo where she became involved in dangerous acting-out behaviors. She ultimately had to leave the country. Finally ending up in New York City, Mai was determined to start a new life. After a period, she made contact with her mother and father, and they, unaware of her lifestyle in Tokyo, were so happy to hear from her that they gladly offered to help her in any way they could.

Since Mai spoke fluent English, she successfully applied to a highly regarded social work program in New York City. After graduating with honors, she took a job at a shelter for homeless women whose histories included psychiatric illness and chemical dependency and began to develop a private practice as a psychotherapist. After a time, Mai met and fell in love with Glen. A daughter was born soon after they married, but the unresolved issues in her past emerged to create serious tensions in their domestic life, and she had difficulty coping with her new life as wife and mother. She was troubled by fear that her husband's attraction to her depended on her willingness to maintain a quiet, diminutive role in their household, just as she had done as a child to avoid exacerbating her mother's trauma. In fact, she had begun to develop a healthy fear of being confined to a passive Audience role in someone else's drama.

During the course of therapy, Mai came to realize that her song-and-dance routine had failed; her husband was not attracted to her Audience-role-based disappearing act. When Mai distanced herself, her husband became worried that she would be unable to assume an equal partnership in the life he wanted them to share. Her husband also refused to accept Mai's resistance to burdening him with her history and emotional issues, instead surprising her with his longing to share as equals in the life-choice of raising a family.

Her explosion was a wake-up call for Mai and her husband. By going into therapy together, they began to see that each had devised behaviors to treat the other based on ideas formed in isolation rather than based on open dialogue and shared experience.

How the Audience Works

The Audience's role may be more primitive than the Performer's role, but it may be the more powerful. Although the Performer's actions are widely varied, the Audience is arguably the role that irrelationship was designed for and is the foundation of the irrelationship process. As we have seen, a Performer is motivated by fear that the world is falling apart. The Audience similarly fears an insecure world in childhood but addresses that fear by tricking the parent into some type of caregiving activity. If that ruse fails, the Audience falls back on a secondary strategy of sneaking away (dissociating) from the relationship when the parent proves unable to provide security. The Audience's absence, then, functions as a protection from the insecurity created by incompetent parenting.

Mai adopted this strategy when her family life became intolerable. And as soon as she was old enough, she fled her family. She learned this behavior early in life when her limbic system, which processes emotions in the brain, learned the withdraw-to-survive strategy to protect herself from her mother's emotional states.

Ironically, the examples in this book may suggest that the Audience is better prepared to manage painful emotions than the Performer. Certainly the Audience's strategy gives more operational space by maintaining distance and blocking connection and empathy. The Audience may, in fact, move from Performer to Performer only barely realizing that each is chronically repeating a song-and-dance routine. And another advantage held by the Audience is that the Performer is often a loose cannon primed to fire accusations against the Audience. The impetus for these accusations is usually the anxiety generated in the Performer when the Audience doesn't satisfactorily fulfill his or her role—usually by failing to show adequate gratitude for the Performer's caretaking. However, the Audience doesn't allow for space to reflect on the part he or she played in the failure of relationships. Conveniently, the Performer's accusations provide ample justification for the Audience to withdraw from the relationship.

Sarah and That Daddy Thing

"I'm always jumping through his hoops," complained Sarah, a woman in her late thirties. "I go to my dad thinking that he wants to help, that he wants to listen to me, and that he cares. But instead he backs down in a weird way and winds up doing that *daddy-thing*." When asked to explain further, Sarah told her therapist the following story.

When she was twenty-five, Sarah's mother was diagnosed with terminal cancer, and it took eight years for her to die. Sarah, a married teaching professional with a small child, moved into the role of primary caretaker for her mother. "In some ways, that was always my role for both of them, Mom and Dad, for as long as I can remember. I wasn't a fixer, though, not really. I was more there to assist, to support, to kind of jump when they asked me to jump."

Although it doesn't sound like it at first pass, Sarah had played Audience to her parents from the get go. "But when I think about it, while I felt like I was doing all that I could for them—to help wherever and whenever I could—my relationship with both of them was really more about playing into this crazy idea they were the ones who were taking care of me— providing care, support, and actually effective parenting."

Because she was at risk for the type of cancer from which her mother died, Sarah sought a genetic counselor who found that she carried high-risk genes. The fear this created was compounded by the memory of her mother's extended illness during which that daddy-thing reared its head in a way that she could not overlook. While her mother was dying, it was part of Sarah's job to make her father feel as if he was actually taking care of Sarah, and her mother, even though he was not. In addition to this, she worried about who would take care of her father, her husband, and her son after she was gone.

Frightened, she found herself on autopilot and called her father. She shared the information she received from the genetic counselor and talked about the anxiety it was causing her. His response was, "Sarah, honey, you are a *good person*." He repeated it a few times in a very soft voice.

At this time, it was her job as Audience to respond to his support as if he were actually being helpful in some way. But Sarah realized that was simply untrue—perhaps always. This recalled for her all the times she went to such great lengths to make her parents feel as if they were helping her.

Not only did his response provide no comfort, but also it brought to mind a chilling memory. During her mother's illness, her father would often say, "Sarah, honey, your mother is a *good person.*" This statement had always confused and angered her.

"What does that have to do with anything?" she asked in therapy. "What is he trying to say? Does he believe that being *good* will *save* anybody or anything? Good? Bad? Who cares? How will *that* make anybody feel better?" She continued to recall the great efforts she went through during her childhood to make her absent parents feel like effective caregivers.

Expressing this in therapy, she added, "Anyway, all I cared about at the time I got the news was whether I was going to be alive or dead." She could not yet ask herself why she expected anything different from her father—something she knew he couldn't deliver—thus setting herself up for further disappointment. That daddy-thing, which she saw herself beginning to play out again now that she needed care and support, was part of an elaborate game she played to help her parents feel better about themselves as parents. Perhaps this routine would even get her father to show up as a *real* father.

Although deeply upset by her father's response, Sarah was compelled initially to continue her song-and-dance routine, pretending her father had provided meaningful support for her. In truth, she continued in her natural state of self-sufficiency to cover up her real feelings. She knew, deep down that the only way she could make herself feel better was by making other people—her father and her husband—feel as if they were helping her. This proved useful as a distraction from her own health concerns and to cover-up her fear that she had no one in her life whom she could count on.

Did Sarah's choice make her feel better? In a way, but that wasn't really the point. That daddy-thing (making someone believe he's an effective caregiver when he isn't) allowed her to worry about one less person. She always felt that her father and mother's relationship was on the verge of falling apart. They, meanwhile, needed to believe that committing to staying together was helpful to her.

Similarly, Sarah felt as if her father would fall apart and stop being her father—which she feared regardless of how low she set the bar for his performance as a parent—if she told him how unhelpful he was now and when her mother was ill.

As she relived this story, the daddy-thing Sarah complained about turned out to be a song-and-dance routine in which her father played a supporting role, with Sarah pretending he was effective. Ironically, his belief that he was useful to his wife and daughter required that he remain in denial of what was really happening to them. Upon examination, Sarah understood that she and her father were in irrelationship and acknowledged she didn't feel close to him. In fact, the idea of being close to him evoked negative feelings related to her mother's death. Although her Audience role distracted her from what she wanted and needed from her father, it also left her feeling lonely. But now that she was aware of her defensive routine, Sarah chose to challenge the status quo with her husband (though not with her father) and confront how they repeated this routine in their everyday life.

Sarah insisted that she and her husband reappraise their relationship. This led them to pull apart their song-and-dance routine and build a relationship in which Sarah felt safe abandoning her isolation so the two of them could face her health issues together.

Finding a Fall Guy or Gal

The Audience is just as entrenched in his or her role as the Performer is, even though the Audience's role deceptively appears to be passive. The Audience's gimmick is to allow the Performer to perform until the disguise slips, revealing that he or she isn't a good person but rather a bad person. This gives the Audience the satisfaction of believing he or she has been the good guy all along.

Think of active and passive forms of aggression. People who operate in a passive-aggressive manner usually get away with it for a while—even at the expense of the actively aggressive Performer who will often escalate into a frenzy of caretaking while the Audience simply watches. A common twist to this behavior is that both parties may be insightful enough to believe that they're receiving due reparations for injuries done to them in childhood, while ignoring their relationship has been stagnating.

The Audience's goal is to find a fall guy or gal to be the star of the relationship—at first. All along, however, the Audience is lying in wait for the Performer to make a mistake so that when something in the relationship goes wrong, the Performer can be blamed. Through all this, each party is using her or his caretaking technique of choice on the other to satisfy his or her own need to feel better.

The Audience's technique originates in the strategy used in childhood to manage the primary caregiver's issues—whether that strategy was to fade into the background to the point of disappearing or to dissociate from family life to manage pain. The Audience's genius lies in managing this strategy so it goes unnoticed. Often the absence of the caregiver sets the stage for the Audience's role, making the child's absence the correct response to the caregiver's absence.

In the case of Mai and her family, Mai correctly understood that her mother needed for Mai to disappear, provided she didn't complain about the lack of parental care or say anything indicating that something was wrong in the family. After she was absent for a time, expressing a desire to see her family became acceptable if such wishes were expressed rarely, meekly, and with no hint of accusation. In truth, Mai was far angrier than she or her family could imagine. In this unspoken agreement, the song-and-dance routine of the Performer is met, step-for-step, by the Audience with an apparently passive but reciprocal routine of her own.

Mary Jo Defibrillates the Defibrillator

Mary Jo came to believe, and for good reason, that her sex appeal worked as a kind of defibrillator for a particular type of lover. At first that's partly why Mary Jo thought, *This was just my kind of challenge*, when her husband, Robert, became depressed. And Robert also knew it to be true, without necessarily knowing that he knew.

Robert's role in his relationship with Mary Jo was to support her need to believe that she could take care of him in every possible sense, which was a replay of the role he acted in his father's life. When Robert was a small child, his father lost his job and his marriage—both probably related to substance abuse—leaving him angry and anxious. His anger acted as a defibrillator for Robert. Throughout his childhood whenever he felt sad or upset reminiscing about his absent mother, his father's tirades pulled him out of his self-pity. And Robert made sure his father knew that his angry outbursts had this medicinal effect on Robert. However, Robert had a hidden agenda; he was terrified that if he let his father know what a terrible parent he was, his father would leave him as his mother had done.

That very same feeling compelled him to incessantly act as if his wife's so-called sex appeal could bring him out of his negative moods. At some level though, Robert had not come to depend upon her as that kind of human antidepressant, the kind of Performer who could kick-start his heart whenever he felt down. But the song-and-dance routines that the two of them played out ensured they would not form an interdependency that would create equality between them, which would result in devastating loss *when*, not *if*, things fell apart.

Mary Jo's father was a successful investment banker, and her mother was an ambitious social climber. They left the heavy lifting of child rearing (Mary Jo and her two older brothers) to an assortment of strangers loosely referred to as "the help." Mary Jo developed complicated sexually seductive routines that worked very well with the teenage California surfer boys in her high school and beyond. Sex had always been a weapon she used to maintain some semblance of control in what otherwise felt like a haphazard life. But, when it came to her parents, these routines were never able to provide any kind of pleasure for, or induce any interest from, her parents, which caused her to redouble her song-and-dance routine to manic, frenzied levels.

Robert, however, was the perfect candidate for her seductive wiles. Throughout the first few years of their relationship, and well into their marriage, Robert was the right kind of nail for the hammer that Mary Jo longed to be. This changed when Robert, in response to a suggestion made by his father who had found recovery through twelve-step meetings, started going to his own twelve-step meetings. Attending the meetings was a game-changer—and a rule-breaker—in Robert's relationship with his wife. "Keep the focus on yourself"—a key slogan in his twelve-step fellowship—proved to be an immense challenge to Robert's unspoken pact regarding his Audience role with his wife who thoroughly depended on him to keep her in an idealized caregiving role.

By keeping the focus on himself and by taking inventory of his contributions to the problems his marriage now faced, Robert realized how his passive caretaking of Mary Jo was fueled, on the surface, by his age-old fear of abandonment that, like his mother, Mary Jo would leave him. Meanwhile Robert was beginning to see that his own song-and-dance routine was a means of creating emotional distance and maintaining control of how much intimacy and emotional risk he allowed himself (and, by extension, Mary Jo) as he played the Audience in irrelationship.

Toward Positive Change

1. **Is it a must that someone takes care of you in a relationship? Describe your needs. Are they really your adult needs or your needs when you were a child? Elaborate.**

2. **Do you find yourself being treated as a child by others? Do you fear confronting this behavior because you're afraid they'll leave you? Provide a few examples from your life.**

3. Have you found that you like being taken care of early in a relationship, but then come to resent it after a while? How do you act out your resentment?

4. Did you sometimes act as if your parents were good and acceptable even when they weren't, just so you could feel safe? Can you describe how you behaved?

5. Looking back at your childhood from an adult perspective, do you remember times when the care you received wasn't what you needed as a child? Do you remember being afraid to ask for anything because you were afraid of upsetting someone or something?

6. Do you sometimes let others believe they are right so the relationship doesn't end? How does that feel?

Part Three
Backstage

The Inner Workings of Irrelationship

Chapter 7

Patterns and Pitfalls

Now that you have a clear understanding of what irrelationship is and how the key players, the Performer and the Audience, remain trapped in their song-and-dance routines to keep life from falling apart, it is time to address some of the mechanics inside the irrelationship that keep it ticking. You will begin to see the possibility of unlocking brainlock and will follow the almost predictable patterns of surreptitious pitfalls, crushing buildups of pain, dissociation, festering resentment, and powerful defenses. Sometimes ecstatic pauses inside the discomfort give the Performer and the Audience the green light that things are working fine. These highs and lows feed irrelationship as more crises come to be expected.

Irrelationship thrives when both players adhere to their scripts. This is the definitive setup for preventing trust, reciprocity, and intimacy to develop. Obviously the implicit agreement is to avoid flexibility that provides space for give and take. Yet individuals who crave closeness create irrelationship. Ultimately, the deep discomfort of isolation and the desire to love and be loved can spark the movement toward healthy change. With commitment and honesty, the armor of irrelationship can be pulled apart, opening the way to recovery.

Escaping Irrelationship: Building Compassionate Empathy

Compassionate empathy is the core principle that allows recovery from irrelationship. Pay attention to the important distinction between compassion and empathy and what they can do when they join forces. *Empathy* is the perception of another person's perspective and experience. It combines intellectual understanding, or *cognitive empathy*, with another person's feelings without the pretense of "I know how you feel."

Compassion is the moral and ethical imperative to take action to change another person's conditions of living in order to reduce their suffering. It requires recognizing and reacting to another person's suffering, which necessitates taking steps to alleviate the suffering. However, compassion does not require the depth of connection and understanding implied by empathy. One can be compassionate while remaining disconnected from the lived experience of the other person. In fact, avoiding an excess of empathy is required to avoid burnout by sustained compassion—a condition sometimes called *compassion fatigue*. Compassion includes compassion for oneself, which prompts us to protect ourselves from over-identifying and losing a sense of proper self-care.

Compassionate empathy juxtaposes empathy and compassion but includes a greater sense of another person's experience. As a shared, relational dynamic, it requires the participation of both people. That is *why* and *how* it is a powerful antidote for the isolation of irrelationship. Simply understanding compassionate empathy takes us beyond empathy to a moral and ethical imperative for both persons to act and change each other's conditions of living—to reduce his or her suffering and yours. Therefore, compassionate empathy is synergistic; it is a force multiplier where empathy leads to compassionate action, and compassion acts as a buffer safeguarding against the risks of over-empathizing—risks such as numbness, burnout, and withdrawal.

Combining compassion and empathy allows us to connect without the complication of our song-and-dance routines. Compassionate empathy is profoundly grounded in reciprocity—it is something we do *with*, not *to*, the people in our lives. Compassionate empathy is the vehicle that takes two or more individuals to a place of safely sharing each other's experiences, especially highly charged emotional issues and problems. This creates a sense of joint ownership of issues encountered without danger to either party.

Without mutuality, empathy can require too much of an individual, causing one to lose his or her sense of self and become overwhelmed, even consumed. This loss, or feared loss, of self is what gave rise to irrelationship in the first place. If a couple steps away from the practice of compassionate empathy, they risk retreating again into irrelationship. Practicing compassionate empathy recalibrates their dynamic by reinforcing skills needed to maintain mutuality.

The Compassionate Empathy Balance

Deficient Empathy	Compassionate Empathy	Excessive Empathy
• Numb • Disconnected • Angry • Indignant • Selfish • Unable to take any perspective other than one's own	• Balances needs between self and others • Reciprocal • Shares the emotional weight of the relationship together • Able to connect without risking getting lost in the other's needs and emotions • Mutuality precludes the need to tune out • Tuned empathy	• Over-connected • Excessive self-sacrifice to the point of self-neglect • Ignores own needs in place of others • Feels hurt, at times traumatized, due to over-identification with others • Unable to take own perspective into account
Irrelationship Audience	**Authentic Relationship**	**Irrelationship Performer**

Intimacy cannot develop without compassionate empathy. Without intimacy, love is in danger of withering or vanishing. Marginalizing the techniques of intimacy may make those within irrelationship feel safe but at the cost of losing the satisfaction and experience of human connection. Commitment to this condition is called brainlock. In brainlock, nothing gets in, nothing gets out, and nothing new is tolerated. Needless to say, empathy and compassion must be completely excluded to maintain brainlock and sustain irrelationship.

People caught in irrelationship seldom become aware of it on their own; they are unaware of choosing irrelationship or of its influence. The gravity of their investment in irrelationship prevents them from realizing that involvement in fixing others' pain is actually a self-centered technique for preventing awareness of their own pain. Discovering and confronting this mechanism is crucial to recovery.

Certain cultural artifacts, especially casual ways of interacting, reinforce maintaining distance. We habitually ask one another, "How you doing? What's happening? What's up?" But we certainly don't expect—don't *want*—an answer, or, at any rate, a meaningful answer. Otherwise, we may have to deal with our neighbor's feelings and experiences, and who has the time for that? These markers of our cultural programming, however, are highly suggestive of our resistance to empathy, and even more, to compassionate empathy.

Anatomy of Defenses

Individuals develop defensive systems to manage potentially overwhelming anxiety, whether the feelings come from inside themselves or from the environment. In the same way that the song-and-dance routine behaviorally isolates the compulsive Performer and Audience from other people, defensive systems always warp the way we see ourselves, in terms of basic identity and what we think we are capable of in work, relationships, and life in general. Like a Trojan horse computer virus, our routines isolate us from ourselves and others, while appearing to bring us together—the perfect deep cover.

Understandably, we cling to our defenses because they work. The problem is that after they've stopped working, we still cling to them out of habit. This is an indicator of conditioned responses reflecting changes in which particular areas of the brain become activated. Flexible neural processing driven by the frontal cortices shifts (anatomically speaking) to areas of the brain such as the ventral striatum, which is associated with more rigid automatic response mechanisms. When this happens, the ability to analyze complex context and events is pushed into the background in favor of unregulated amygdala activity so that the ability to mount nuanced responses to emotions, such as fear, is dampened or lost.

Looking at these mechanisms a little more closely, researchers wanted to know if lonely people responded differently to strangers as compared to people close to them. Subjects were shown images of strangers and people close to them to see if loneliness was significantly correlated with differences in ventral-striatum activity. They found that when lonely people viewed people close to them, but not strangers, their ventral striatum was more active, suggesting that the possibility of intimacy induced a greater drive to try to reconnect.

People in irrelationship are caught in a destructive situation in which they are pulled in multiple directions at once, i.e., being psychologically and relationally drawn and quartered. When unconsciously pushing others away and consolidating their isolation and loneliness, they are, at the same time, driven to seek closeness and intimacy. When two (or more) people in irrelationship are doing a variation of the same thing, the situation is even more complex.

The process of recovery includes recuperating the ability to identify, examine, and disempower defenses in order to create enough time and mental space for self-reflection and to leverage the brain's neuroplastic capacity to develop alternative strategies for dealing with anxiety in oneself and in relationships, thereby building greater resilience.

Our defenses are so powerful that they can

- limit self-awareness;
- condition how we relate to others;
- influence how we make choices; and
- end up costing more than they save.

High anxiety strengthens defenses by

- impairing higher brain functions;
- reducing the ability of the brain to respond flexibly, i.e., lowering plasticity;
- increasing the use of automatic reactive patterns; and
- causing anxiety to increase in people around us.

Because the defenses of both Performer and Audience developed in a social environment, new approaches are best learned in a social environment. A broadened context will demand a different adaptation from the old song-and-dance routine and will help Performer and Audience unlearn bad habits and misperceptions and relearn flexibility and openness. Psychotherapy is a useful environment for initiating and strengthening this practice.

Bonnie Tries to Outthink Her Feelings

"Do you think when he finally throws me out I will be alone for the rest of my life?" asked Bonnie, a middle-aged woman who had been dating a much younger man.

"No," her therapist gently but frankly answered. "There are far too many wounded birds out there who need your help. Besides, he's yet another one who seems to relish the safety of being with a woman who requires so little of him—no demand for intimacy, in fact, you come with no demands at all."

Silence. As consternation and anger passed quickly over Bonnie's face, tears followed.

"I have never been with a man who was not ultimately abusive," she said quietly.

"Never?"

"No, not never, now that I think about it. My first husband, Matt, he loved me. He would never hurt me. He wanted us to have children and be happy. He lived to serve me."

"What happened to him?"

"I couldn't take it. It all felt too alien and unfamiliar. He seemed so needy. He wanted to know me. That certainly wasn't going to happen. I ruined that marriage. I was the insane one then. I was abusive toward him. Everyone else I've been with has hurt me, but for some reason I always felt safe with them."

Bonnie's story highlights an important theme. You can't outthink your feelings. Whether we like it or not—or are aware of it or not—our feelings show up in our behavior and interaction patterns, especially with people who are closest to us. This is especially true about feelings of discomfort, stress, anger, fear, or any emotional state we think of as unacceptable. And it doesn't make the slightest difference whether the feeling is reasonable or rational. All that matters is that we're feeling it. Not wanting to be known by oneself and others worsens the problem by creating mental blind spots leading to contradiction and confusion because we are being influenced by powerful feelings we are trained to ignore.

Bonnie and her therapist worked through a series of her failed relationships that revealed what her feelings were and how she played them out romantically. In a long line of repetitive ostensibly intimate, romantic relationships with Audiences, Performer Bonnie consistently sought, cornered, captured, and fixed the most difficult-to-treat men. And so long as Bonnie remained willing to continue to fix the men she encountered, she didn't need to worry about any one of them turning on her—turning to face her, emotionally, and actually wanting to know her intimately. Through the song-and-dance routines that she enacted with her partners, she wound up protecting herself from those things which she herself had never accepted and which she unconsciously could not know about herself. Anyone who genuinely wanted to know her, to share life and live with her, had to be obliterated and expelled from her life because—by accepting her as she is—he would upset the balance by refusing to create brainlock with her. And that acceptance is what intimacy is all about.

Part of Bonnie, however, wanted to end the madness associated with the impossible task her feelings compelled her to undertake, driving her to jump into the next irrelationship almost immediately after being thrown out by the last incurable patient, whom she sometimes called "boyfriend" or "husband." With the help of her therapist and the acceptance she was beginning give to herself, Bonnie was building empathy, allowing intimacy into her life. Perhaps the fact that she was being taken care of by another person, the therapist, was the beginning of the end for her defensive systems; she turned them upside down.

Bonnie was able to recover something that her well-honed dissociation had blocked out. We all need to be known. Human beings have a biologically based need to be known by other people and by oneself; it is required for emotional and physical survival and is wired into us from before birth. When a distorted survival mechanism to prevent our being known is in place, such as a caregiver's conveying to a child that his or her needs are greater than the child's, this creates a double bind, confusing our need to be cared for and protected with a compulsion to care for and protect. Being freely known is disallowed in irrelationship. However, our feelings and deep needs demand expression and categorically won't allow themselves to be denied or outthought indefinitely.

Sympathy, Empathy, and Intimacy

A significant aspect of the irrelationship system is the substitution of sympathy for empathy, which is similar to mistaking pity for compassion. One of Bonnie's key insights on her road to recovery is how she had chosen man after man, in large part, based on how sorry she felt for him. She realized, in treatment, that this was sympathy, not empathy. Empathy requires far more emotional and mental work than distant, safer, and sometimes even patronizing sympathy—like patting someone on the head. Empathy is the profoundly intimate experience of another person's feelings by recalling one's own experience of the same or similar feelings—an experience irrelationship is designed to prevent.

With this in mind, let's return to Bonnie, who recalls conversations with her current partner, Max, and her ex-husband, Matt—who threatened actual intimacy—to illustrate the difference in content, feeling, and tone between sympathy and empathy.

Max: Listen, Dear, I'm sorry that I was unable to make it to your performance; I was just so upset about losing my job. I am so disappointed in myself. I thought, this time, that I'd be able to be, you know, a contributor in our relationship.

Bonnie: I know, I know—I figured something like that had happened, Max. You know that I love and accept you just the way you are.

Max: So you're not mad at me? You're not going to throw me out?

Bonnie: No, I've already said so, a thousand times: I love you just the way you are.

Max: My God, you treat me so well. I just hope that someday I can repay you for all that you've done for me.

Of course, as a Performer, Bonnie wouldn't hear of it. In this conversation, Bonnie once again lets a would-be lover off the hook. By sympathizing with his disappointment, she lets both of them get away with having zero demands—or even low level requirements—except to not threaten each other with actual intimacy. It worked.

As Bonnie went into the details of her conversation with Max, she was able to see how she used sympathy to avoid holding him accountable for his behavior, his commitment to their relationship, and his presence in her life—in other words, a conversation where she skirted the threat of empathy. This revelation, however, brought to mind one of the final conversations she had with her ex-husband.

Matt: Bonnie, I have felt so sad lately; I feel you pulling away, and I want, I need, to know what's making you feel so distant.

Bonnie: It's nothing, Matt. You're imagining things—I'm fine, we're okay. I promise, everything is okay.

Matt: I know *that's* not true, Bonnie. Why won't you let me in? We have shared so much. You told me how other men have treated you, and I promised you that I would not hurt you. Now that we've come this close, don't you think that I know when you're shutting me out?

Bonnie: Your accusation that I'm shutting you out, Matt, that *is* what's hurting me. Why won't you leave me alone?

In this conversation, Matt uses empathy, his willingness to access his own feelings of care, affection, and vulnerability, to reach the woman he loves. It's risky considering how adverse his wife would be to the resulting intimacy if she were to open up. But he correctly senses that it's a waste of time to try to reach his wife, who has already checked out of their relationship. Bonnie counters his empathy by turning the tables on him, aggressively defending that, through empathy, she has already opened up herself to a too costly emotional investment in the man who had almost succeeded in reaching her. Not long after this, Matt became unable to tolerate the distance between him and the woman he loved but felt painfully estranged from—even though they slept in the same bed.

Joe and Dr. Smith Explore Empathy

"I don't know what's wrong," said Dr. Smith, a therapist. "After about a year of surprisingly productive work with Joe, the whole process seems to have bogged down."

"Why surprisingly?" Dr. Smith's supervisor asked.

Dr. Smith began describing how, about a year into his therapy, Joe began to open up about what might be the real reason for his coming into treatment. He originally agreed, although reluctantly, to come into therapy when his partner Manny told him that if he didn't, he, Manny, was going to leave. Manny was no longer willing to live with someone who was so distant and closed off. Since Joe's treatment was forced (not the best setup for successful therapeutic outcomes), neither Joe nor his therapist felt particularly invested in it.

What was surprising, Dr. Smith told his supervisor, was that Joe was beginning to do the real work in therapy without having intended to do so. Dr. Smith initially felt some objective sympathy for Joe but had not really been present for Joe in a genuinely empathetic way. But Joe's progress was now beginning to demand it.

Sensing the lack of genuine investment and empathy from his therapist, Joe emotionally boycotted his therapy, which made the ticking away of the forty-five-minute sessions increasingly intolerable. But one day, out of the blue, Joe started talking about the terrible accident his father suffered when Joe was twelve years old. The accident severely crippled him, effectively bringing to an end his role as head of the household and breadwinner. Even with multiple surgeries and around-the-clock care, he would never function independently again.

The accident instantly transformed Joe's family life. His mother, who was a Latin-American immigrant, suddenly changed from housewife and mother to full-time caregiver for an invalid. Joe's role also changed dramatically as he became second-in-command of the household. This included his becoming caretaker of his caregiver-mother. Although Joe didn't know it at the time, this experience created and hardened a resolution in him never to be trapped in such a situation ever again.

Manny was Joe's third boyfriend to make the threat that he would leave if Joe didn't start to show up for their relationship. At last, Joe accepted the challenge.

Dr. Smith found himself confronted by a similar challenge. His supervisor advised him that if he was going to provide meaningful care for Joe, he was going to have to get into the game with Joe rather than watching from the bleachers. So he took the challenge and recalibrated his approach to Joe's therapy.

At first nothing seemed out of the ordinary about Joe's next session with Dr. Smith—but Dr. Smith failed to realize the impact his supervisor had on him. Having agreed that his relationship with Joe needed to change, he unconsciously moved from a posture of self-protecting, sympathetic distance to one of openhearted empathy toward his client. During the session, without warning, Dr. Smith felt a sudden pain in his stomach. His own tears began to well up as Joe described in detail what it had been like for him to lose both his parents to his father's work accident and its aftermath.

Dr. Smith began to feel terrible feelings of loss—but not Joe's loss. Through his empathic connection with Joe, Dr. Smith relived the sudden, overwhelming death of his own grandmother, who took on the role of his caregiver during his mother and father's frequent travels. Thirty years later, he, like Joe, unexpectedly found himself mourning a devastating childhood loss. Dr. Smith's new willingness to experience his own pain finally made him available to Joe in the way Joe needed him to be.

Why did Dr. Smith, and not Joe, feel this emotional transition as a gut punch? Simply because Joe had been unaware of his pain and sadness until Dr. Smith's reconnection to his own experience provided a safe, empathic environment in which Joe could allow himself to feel. This new connection created a space that could hold the unbearable emotions each felt for himself and for the other person.

"I can't help believing that some of the sadness that I'm feeling in my heart, some of it," said Dr. Smith, "belongs to you." In response, Joe wept—and wept—for the first time in decades.

From the safety of uninvested, objective sympathy, Dr. Smith had been able to tell Joe in earlier sessions how bad he felt for him. When their exchange crossed into empathy, however, Dr. Smith relived his own pain, which enabled him to join Joe in *his* pain. The experience of empathy unlocked frightening areas of uncertainty and vulnerability, allowing both Joe and his therapist to be known by another person.

What Is Intimacy?

As seen in Bonnie's conversation with Matt and the ongoing empathic connection between Dr. Smith and Joe, *intimacy* is the emotional connection between two people that allows sharing what we feel, think, and do with someone with whom we are in the process of actually living our lives on a committed, regular basis. Intimacy is a felt and lived experience of closeness with another person, so that to a significant degree they are involved in one another's private world. It allows sharing of the admirable, the reprehensible, and the humiliating. But intimacy is not what happens as a result of rapidly telling the intimate partner everything; it's the unfolding and sharing of life that comes about as partners learn the gradually and vulnerably revealed truths about one another, staying and growing together through that process. Intimacy transcends the individuals in a relationship and becomes a form that relationships settle into after a long and circuitous process.

Relationships created from the defensive posture of irrelationship have no room for intimacy because intimacy threatens the stability of the irrelationship pattern. So for all the energy put into a song-and-dance routine, the only gratification it can deliver is relief for the participants from being asked to examine themselves and each other too closely. This leaves the irrelationship participants prey to feeling ripped off by each other, which is a setup for blaming—either oneself or one's partner. This is one reason why compassion and empathy are important; they provide tools that can help eliminate the need for retaliation. On a deeper level, research has shown that compassion improves the ability of the brain to reconfigure itself to more positive modes of conflict resolution,[1] although empathy without the more rational guidance of compassion carries risks of its own, as will be discussed in a later chapter. This reconfiguration is reflected in changes in patterns of brain activity as well as in reorganization on the cellular level, including, in some cases, increased size of the areas of the brain associated with mindful and compassionate functioning.

As suggested earlier, the isolation and dissatisfaction that arises from irrelationship paradoxically results from using words and gestures that pass for empathy while the user of these gestures keeps a safe emotional distance from the object. Everybody believes they're trying to do the right thing but nothing's working, and nobody knows why.

Confused and Feeling Ripped Off: Signs of Change

Humans are equipped with a capacity for empathy and compassion that goes beyond the ability to do good deeds or do what we're supposed to do. Without empathy, our world is a self-created fantasy in which we imitate feelings according to behaviors we observe in others or, more distantly, see in movies or television—we feign what we're supposed to feel while ignoring what we actually feel. In the same way, our connection with others will be only an imitation of behaviors we observe between people we believe are genuinely connected with one another.

Imitation is facilitated by the mirror neurons, discussed in Chapter 5, and is a key to children's socialization as well as our (and other species') learning from one another. Usually, evolution has made imitation a good thing. For example, when an ape learns how to access a kind of food, another ape observes and absorbs this new knowledge, which rapidly spreads through the group.

In irrelationship, the ease with which we learn by imitation becomes perverted, so that unhelpful knowledge spreads like wildfire. Artificially constructed behaviors actually deepen our mystified isolation from others. And yet, we know down deep that something is wrong but can't put our finger on what it is. But rather than voicing our confusion and seeking help, we repress our feelings of confusion, thus denying ourselves information that can help us out of this labyrinth.

As mentioned earlier, a common characteristic of irrelationship is feeling ripped off because one party gives more than he or she gets—or believes this to be the case. This is true for both the Performer and the Audience, although the Performer's giving is more covert and blatant. Neither player connects this routine with the tricks they learned as children to make their caregiver feel better and their world feel safer. In this situation, heated emotions, such as anger and anxiety, prevent higher brain centers from functioning well, resulting in impatience, irritation, and an impaired ability to think reflectively. Moreover, these heated emotions "hijack" the brain's amygdala,[2] thus interfering with the ability to evaluate what's happening objectively and put a stop to it.

The growing dissatisfaction Performer and Audience live with is the breakthrough pain of feeling that the routine isn't working so well anymore. They're no longer doing such a good job of juggling the conflicted feelings that accompany being either Performer or Audience. While it may not feel good at the time, this pain is a window of opportunity for both the Performer and Audience to realize the jig is up.

Toward Positive Change

1. Define and distinguish between compassion and empathy.

2. Describe your experience of compassion and empathy in important relationships, current or past.

3. Explain the role compassion can have in managing empathy to prevent a person from becoming immobilized by exaggerated emotional states.

Chapter 8

A Funny Thing Happened on the Way to Adulthood

Unlocking brainlock is a daunting challenge to the Performer and the Audience who have well-worked-out rules about what is and is not allowed to happen in their relationship. Each player seems to provide what the other needs, but all hell breaks loose if one person changes the rules. The crisis arising from a change in each person's script can result in instant feelings of neglect, anger, or both, leading to threats of abandonment and brain activity that stop the development of insight into what's actually going on between them.

Steve and Laura's Game of Chicken

"I'm leaving," Steve screams at Laura.

"Oh yeah? Not if I beat you to the door, you're not," Laura yells back.

Perhaps this sounds like a standoff between former lovers whose relationship has entered its terminal phase. But don't be fooled; it's just another rehearsal in this couple's song-and-dance routine. It's not a credible threat of suicide for the relationship because they clearly aren't going to break up and yet need to keep saying they will—a signal that help is needed. They do have a chance to say, "What are the rules?" and "Let's change them."

When they become willing to change the rules, they are on their way to recovery, but that's not in the cards quite yet.

In reality, Steve, the Performer, and Laura, the Audience and sometime Performer, are frustrated and dysfunctionally elated because once again they have met their match in one another. Each is threatening to withdraw from their part in the song-and-dance routine—to stop administering the treatment for the problem that each sees in the other. And each sincerely believes that if the other would admit to having the problem and surrender to treatment, everything would be fine.

Dan and Jolene introduced Steve and Laura and believed the relationship would be a match made in heaven, and it seemed so for a short while. But disappointment overtook Steve and Laura after about three months together. Instead of withdrawing amicably, they sealed themselves in their misery by continuing to perform for Dan and Jolene as if they were still that match made in heaven. Why? They had prematurely bonded for life; their attachment system was setup to catch-and-keep like a relational mousetrap. Their song-and-dance routines clicked into place, and all the dials soared to the red zone of irrelationship.

Steve was thrilled to get into Harvard Business School where he met and became friends with Dan. Both came from middle-class Irish-Catholic families, growing up on opposite ends of Long Island, and were enthusiastic New York Jets fans. Each did well at the prestigious financial institution where both had gotten jobs. Steve's success enabled him to send money to his parents to help them on occasion.

Steve pushed himself at work, putting in a lot of overtime, driving himself through relationship after unsuccessful relationship with women, never able to find "the one." His friend Dan, on the other hand, met Jolene and fell in love, got married, had two children, and bought a house on Long Island.

Laura and Jolene came from upper-middle class families in Little Rock. Laura recalled that her father's business absorbed so much of his time that he was never home. Her mother stayed home and became a housewife. The oldest of three girls, Laura went to work for a health insurance company in Little Rock, secretly fearing she would never be able to leave home as she watched her best friend move to New York City. Laura and Jolene were both thrilled when Laura's company transferred her to New York City.

Before they met, Steve and Laura had each told Dan and Jolene how much they admired their marriage. This prompted Jolene to suggest to Dan that they might instigate a meeting between Steve and Laura. The four of them met in a Manhattan restaurant, and little time passed before all four were aware of the chemistry between Steve and Laura. At the end of the evening, Laura told Jolene on the quiet that Steve was "really something."

Almost immediately, Steve and Laura became inseparable. The excitement kept them up late every night as they went out, made plans, and introduced each other to friends and family members. Steve often told Dan that this was "the real deal."

Problems first surfaced in what appeared to be a minor tug-of-war about which of the two was doing more for the other; that is, which was the Performer and which the Audience. Both felt they detected in the other a familiar lack of appreciation that had undermined past relationships. After three months the honeymoon was over.

Steve enjoyed behaving chivalrously toward the women he dated but found that to many women this read as controlling or dominating. His take on this was that they simply didn't get that he was just trying to be helpful.

In Laura's experience, the men with whom she had been involved in the past often reached a point at which they would say to her, "Hey, you're not my mother." Sometimes her helpfulness led to her being called a nag or a harpie. Laura's feeling was that the men who reacted this way were either narrow-minded or not smart enough to recognize a good thing, "even if it bit them on the butt."

After three months of these colliding sensibilities, Steve and Laura no longer felt as if their match was made in heaven. From the outside looking in, we can easily see that the brainlock of irrelationship was holding them together—or apart. Both knew that a good relationship takes work, but they were awash in self-righteousness before they'd even had a chance to get to know each other. They found good opponents in one another with whom they could contend against the injustice they'd faced in the past.

For individuals not looking for escape into irrelationship, this would have signaled that something was wrong. Since Steve and Laura were each primed developmentally to misperceive relationships in the characteristic ways we have been discussing, they missed crucial signals and maintained their collision course. But it was the perfect environment for repeating painful family dramas. At first both felt isolated in their relationship, which drove them to keep doing for the other despite the frustration of not receiving the recognition they wanted.

By the time Steve and Laura went into therapy, they were approaching the first anniversary of their game of chicken. Instead of seeing who will veer off first, Steve and Laura were caught in the brainlock of irrelationship, forcing their helpfulness on one another but too full of self-respect to violate the rules of their song-and-dance routine. The threats of leaving periodically lobbed at one another are essential to the routine, like cars speeding toward one another in a game of chicken. But Steve and Laura have confused ideas about love as well as retaliatory anger and the inability to face one's own vulnerability. As they continue to engage, their game becomes so entangled that they can't see where one part of the routine ends and the other begins.

Separating their so-called love from the threat and rage had become almost impossible. They were locked into a view of themselves, and each other, that for years simply did not leave room for that most essential ingredient for recovery from the isolation and defensiveness of irrelationship: willingness—a willingness to grow, to change, with no guarantee, and to accept ourselves and our partners as we are.

Going into therapy together is a certain sign of hope in the face of irrelationship. As Steve and Laura's therapy went forward this small amount of hope did grow into the willingness to identify their irrelationship trap and to recover from it.

The Promise of a Chink in the Armor

By now it will be apparent that irrelationship does not make its participants better adjusted or happier. In fact, the successful Performer, in particular, believes that he or she has fixed the Audience and is saving the relationship, and is, therefore, committed to keeping things from changing. This is confirmed and maintained by activity in the brain that holds the individual to established, familiar reactions and behaviors, stabilized within patterns of secure attachment. Stress from outside that threatens, or even questions, the pattern results in causing the individual to increase resolve, making the pattern even more rigid and harder to unlearn. However, this brittle rigidity is a poor cover for the fear and isolation the Performer and the Audience live in and with, which leads to that vague unease felt by people living in irrelationship.

However, failure is not consciously considered an option. Those committed to irrelationship are thoroughly committed to the good, the bad, and the ugly of their song-and-dance routine. The following chart illustrates the hopelessness underlying the choices available to those in irrelationship.

Irrelationship: The Good, The Bad, and The Ugly

The Good	The Bad	The Ugly
My anxiety is relieved.	Something doesn't feel quite right.	I'm by myself and depressed.
My routine is working.	I'm not getting the right response to my routine.	No one appreciates me. I'm left holding the bag.

As can be seen, good isn't really good. When irrelationship is working, an open experience of life and love are categorically excluded. Being able to feel bad is what is actually *good*. The true experience of emotion—*any* emotion, including loneliness, fear, or fury—puts your song-and-dance routine on notice that it's near its final act. But this is not failure; this is the beginning of the end of brainlock, and you can finally get out of the irrelationship trap.

No doubt, the familiar trap of irrelationship can snag you again. Familiar old feelings and signals can be seductive and again can try to take you down the pathway of devaluing and distancing yourself from others so you feel better. If you've read this far, though, you've already started to know what was familiar didn't work. Consciously, we all need to live as if the ground under our feet will bear our weight—to believe that the world can be a secure, stable, and just place in which we can live.

A Just World?

The idea—an assumption even—that the world is supposed to be fair, or just,[1] is ingrained in us from our earliest years; parents teach us to be fair to others in and near our family. Later, we learn that our teachers and peers have similar expectations in the classroom and on the playground. Still later in the workplace, we encounter contracts, codes of conduct, policies, and procedures which employees are expected to adhere. Last, but certainly not least, a major branch of our government was instituted to enforce fairness, or justice, for all citizens, ostensibly without respect to socioeconomic standing or other considerations. All of these examples are the outward and visible signs of a cultural commitment to ideas of justice intended to condition all of our dealings with one another, thus keeping the world safe and orderly for everyone.

As observed earlier, the need to feel safe is the principal driver of irrelationship. This implies the need for a place to lay blame when things go awry causing the individual to feel unsafe. However, the distinctive histories of people in relationships makes them prone to place blame on *themselves* when things go wrong—even in situations where they have little or no direct relationship. How does this happen in a culture with such high regard for the ideas of justice and fair play?

The answer to this apparent contradiction lies in a self-deception created by the child when the caregiver's negative moods began to cause him or her to feel that the world is unsafe. The child learned the rules for keeping the caregiver happy, so the child felt safe before he or she was developmentally capable of grasping what learning was. This blindly operating mechanism is carried forward through childhood and adolescence and into adulthood.

In these circumstances, where does the child place blame for the things in his or her environment that are frightening? Since the child has already unconsciously disregarded the caregiver as a source to lay blame, the only remaining choice is to blame him- or herself. Unhappily, once this mechanism goes live, the child will habitually use it, keeping it close at hand to secure a just explanation for negative events and stimuli.

However, identifying an acceptable target for blame is not the totality of what occurs when a child adopts this strategy. Explaining painful experiences by blaming oneself also initiates changes in the synaptic development in the child's brain so that self-blame becomes a fundamental component of his or her operating system, and it crucially conditions how the child analyzes the world. This type of behavior is observable in the child's understanding of areas, such as

- how people treat themselves and one another;
- how to process and discuss feelings (or not);
- how reward and punishment are administered and perceived;
- how safe or dangerous the world is and how this may be managed; and
- how the acceptability and efficacy of related adaptation techniques are taken up later in life.

So how is this worked out in the conscious and unconscious mind of the child—and later as an adult—in day-to-day life? In basic terms, a child would say, "I *must* believe in the fairness of the world in order to be able to survive and live in the world. Mom keeps me safe, warm, and fed. The idea that she could be unfair is unthinkable, so if she's upset, angry, or even abusive, it must be my fault." For the child, any other explanation is not only impermissible but also unintelligible.

Now imagine a child whose mother is a "rage-a-holic"—someone who loses control regularly, throws things, and even hits the child. How does this child manage a mother like this? Since the child believes the mother's volatility is his or her fault, the only available tool for fixing it is to fix his or her own behavior. So the child locks down his or her behavior and learns to walk a tightrope, changing the behavior in any possible way in order to maintain the belief that the world is fair and manageable. However, it gets even more complicated; the child's rigid approach to the caregiver and his or her own behavior ultimately makes flexibility impossible and leaves the child unable to accept the reality that everyone makes mistakes—including the child.

As the child goes through life, he or she will apply this early programming to interactions with everyone, regardless of relationship or circumstances. Intimacy becomes virtually impossible because, based on the earliest unsettling encounters with the mother, the child's brain activity was channeled along fear-based circuits (the brain's ventral processing) with little activity in areas of the brain that accommodate context-sensitivity (the brain's dorsal processing). As a result, virtually every person and situation encountered in life is treated as a crisis in which a sense of urgency displaces the capacity for judgment even in cases when time is available for deliberation and considered response.

This technique of crisis management, resulting from a perceived need to keep the world from falling apart, remains below the radar throughout the child's life and conditions every interaction with others through adulthood. Without intervention, the person locked into this attitude toward the world is unlikely ever to grasp the unspoken deal that was made with his or her mother and how it cripples the ability to be in the moment with another person.

When the Song-and-Dance Routine Stops Working

By this time, you may have begun to accept that something needs to change, although the prospect is frightening and may seem impossible because the song-and-dance routine has protected you for years. The idea of living without your routine may almost cause panic because on some level you realize that the anxiety you and your partner have long kept neatly tucked away has begun to surface. However, three crucial things have changed since the routine was first created:

- As an adult, your social and coping skills are better, more flexible, and more extensive than the skills available to you as a frightened child.

- Having lived as an adult in society and having developed broader emotional and cognitive capacities, you are able to grasp that your caregiver—whether as a child or as an adult—is not the total of your world.

- The isolation in which you live is no longer the result of being a frightened child. Your experience in the world brings you into contact with people who show genuine interest and caring about your wellbeing. As an adult, others expect you to exercise self-determination that isn't subordinate to the wishes and desires of others.

Based on these factors, you may be on the road to putting aside the song-and-dance routine in favor of recovery.

How Can I Be Sure?

As discussed previously, windows of opportunity for recognizing the possibility of change can and do appear even when irrelationship is in full flower. But what do these windows look like?

Basically, a window of opportunity is a moment of insight or clarity that allows us to see our routine for what it is: a defense against true human connection. Often these windows of opportunity appear during moments of fear of loss or pain while interacting with our intimate partner or another person close to us. It's much like the experience of the addict who has hit bottom and thinks he or she can't, or doesn't want to, go any deeper—sometimes called being "sick and tired of being sick and tired."

Examples of experiences that may be recognized as a bottom are

- loss of an important relationship, such as a marriage or long-standing friendship;
- loss of a job;
- misreading social cues resulting in a humiliating blunder;
- sudden, inexplicable conflict with someone whom we believed everything was fine; and
- sudden distancing by someone who we've long depended on or been good to.

In all of these cases, someone or something we've depended on has suddenly been removed. Sometimes it's the result of one of the involved parties breaking a rule of the irrelationship. But also it can be the result of song-and-dance fatigue, causing one party to realize it's just not working, so he or she just steps away—not really knowing what that means or how to deal with it.

Lucy Steps through a Window of Opportunity

Year after year, Lucy, a thirty-three-year-old stockbroker who grew up in Austin, Texas, would return to New York City depressed from her holiday trip home to see her parents. Back in therapy, she'd express more insight into the anxiety—bordering on terror—which she always felt in the presence of her overbearing and dominant father. Almost invariably and even against her will, Lucy would at least partly revert to her childhood role as if she had never left home.

When she first started going to her parents for the holidays, she would bring her father expensive gifts to bribe him into being nice to her. But, over the years, Lucy decreased the lavishness of her gifts, feeling less and less willing to buy off her father.

For some reason during this particular year, Lucy had agreed, at the request of her younger sister who still lived in Austin, to share the cost of a particularly expensive gift for their father. Lucy knew some, but not all, of the details about the foul moods her father had been suffering from over the last year. She was sorry for him despite her wariness of being around him and genuinely wanted to help him feel better.

After a lot of effort and planning, Lucy and her sister somehow managed to convince their parents to stay at their older sister's house during Christmas week. Meanwhile, they had the whole kitchen in their parents' house renovated, costing thousands of dollars. At the end of the week, they all returned to the house together, including Lucy's brother-in-law and three children.

"Close your eyes, Daddy," Lucy shouted as they entered the new kitchen.

He walked in, opened his eyes, and said—nothing.

The backstory that finally emerged was her father and sister had tricked Lucy. Her father, in league with her sister, had designed the new kitchen himself and kept the secret, fooling Lucy into believing an entirely different storyline.

As Christmas Day wore on, Lucy's father's mood deteriorated. He began whining and complaining that no one cared about him anymore. Finally Lucy's sister leveled with her and told her that their father was impossible to please and bitter about everything. His anxiety bordered on panic. He had finally gone into therapy and was taking anti-anxiety medication.

When Lucy returned to New York, she complained to her therapist, "They didn't tell me anything about this." She felt resentful, betrayed, and stupid. But she also felt anger about the years and money she had spent vainly trying to please her father.

And then, after all those years of the same thing, Lucy said, "I fell for it again. I couldn't resist the temptation. I keep thinking I can do something to make my father feel better. When will I learn? It never works."

Lucy finally worked on establishing boundaries between herself and her family, particularly, her father. She could talk about feeling betrayed and acknowledge the ways that her behavior contributed to her own suffering. After taking these giant steps in her therapy, she began to view herself and her family with newfound compassion.

For most of her life, Lucy jumped through every hoop her father put in front of her and got better at it each time. But the more effort she spent to satisfy his demands, the tighter the hoops got. Finally the day came when Lucy realized she couldn't fit through the hoops anymore and gave up the idea of even trying. She surrendered and resigned from the job of fixing her father. To her unimaginable surprise, she began to feel free. This was Lucy's window of opportunity. Luckily for Lucy, she saw it for what it was and stepped through.

Occasionally through a window of opportunity, a Performer or Audience catches a glimpse of a breathtakingly different idea of who he or she is and how interaction with others should occur. Breakthroughs of unaccustomed emotions, such as pain, fear, or sadness, can allow the Performer, Audience, or both an instantaneous new perception of relationships and the roles they want to act out in them. Long-standing barriers of stored resentments and self-righteousness may suddenly begin to break apart, revealing the couple's sadness and loneliness. They may even wonder if they ever really liked one another in the first place.

The predetermined roles of irrelationship don't leave space for extreme emotions—or perhaps for any emotions at all. If extreme emotions are allowed any time, this could be an indication that the players have stepped aside from their roles, if only briefly. This may sound like disaster for the couple, perhaps even death of the relationship. However, the novelty of such a moment can be a window of opportunity that, if recognized, can be used to take a strike against brainlock. Instantaneously and automatically, such emotion can provide insight that can rapidly undermine the distancing upon which the irrelationship depends.

Although not commented upon as such, this book has already presented several examples of couples who stumbled into windows of opportunity and used them to create change.

- Sam and Claire (Chapter 4): Sam felt that he had taken a kick in the groin when their couples' therapist told the infinitely giving Performer that he was selfish by not allowing Claire to give to him, thus disallowing her to have real value to him.

- Carol and Kate (Chapter 5): Kate refused to be force-fed by Carol, and this provided a moment where the two of them could see—and feel—how they'd been enslaved by their old family dynamics to play out and recreate a routine together that ensured they would pass by each other, without the threat of intimacy.
- Mary Jo and Robert (Chapter 6): Robert invited Mary Jo through a window of opportunity by refusing to jump through the hoops that she had set out for him, as the Performer, and by allowing herself to take in the value of a partner who loved her for more than her sexual appeal—breaking a lifelong pattern of isolation for both.
- Dr. Smith and Joe (Chapter 7): Dr. Smith and Joe were in a perfect position—the therapy was forced—to avert the window of opportunity that opened for them and to avoid the hard work of actual empathy instead of the sympathy that Dr. Smith had shown Joe. But when they shared a pain that was essential to Joe's therapy process, they chose to step through the window of opportunity together.

Prepare to look for with windows of opportunity in your life. Chapter 9 will provide guidance for being ready when it happens. Not everyone is able to see the window of opportunity for what it is or, having seen it, is ready to step through. But as you read, you'll learn how to create them for yourself.

Sunny and Tom Get a Shot

What happens when one member of a couple breaks the contract? What happens when one member spots that window of opportunity and makes a big shift?

Tom is a Performer, and Sunny is his Audience. These roles have served them well for years. After the birth of their second child, the diabetes that Sunny's doctors had associated with her pregnancy (gestational diabetes) did not go away as it had after their first child's birth. Tom was more than happy to perform the doctor role. In the beginning, Sunny was fine with playing the Audience as his patient.

After a couple of years of Tom supervising the treatment effectively, Sunny found herself sick of it. She had been quite able to comply with the treatment regimen, the one the real doctors had prescribed, on her own. But her medical condition had caused Tom such extreme stress that Sunny had accepted his "perfectionism," which is what they had been calling it. But things suddenly changed for Sunny, and she began to see him as imperfect, controlling, and impossible to live with. She started to feel she didn't want his help all of the time. Since Tom was the quintessential Performer, he could not ramp down his scrupulously conscientious treatment, so he went from perfect to failure.

Tom's pride was wounded. Feeling that he'd failed made him try to manipulate his wife back into the role of disabled patient (Audience) so he could continue to feel successful. But Sunny had been doing a bit of self-examination and had begun to explore the contours and the limitations of her Audience role—a role that caused her to play the victim, which she could no longer stand. Anyway, Sunny had Tom's number and was no longer willing to play the victim for the sake of his ego.

Tom got stuck in his song-and-dance routine—without necessarily knowing it himself—and was losing his Audience. Working his way out of this situation was going to be difficult. He assumed he could impose his Performer behavior on his willing Audience again, and things would fall back into place. But Sunny was no longer interested.

Tom told her, "Look, I agree with you; I am hard on myself, but look at your condition. I have to be perfect or you will die, making me a total failure."

Sunny saw the window of opportunity and had a choice to make. She refused to regress to her old song-and-dance routine and comply with her perpetual patient role to make Tom feel good. When she refused, both she and Tom suddenly felt a powerful wave of the anxiety that had driven their irrelationship for years. Miraculously, Tom woke up to his pain and fear, and they were able, together, to help each other stay out of their old song-and-dance routine. Out poured the emotions they'd been trying to strangle, especially the deep fear of loving and losing one another. But they also opened up to a closeness that was built upon facing their fears together. They felt, finally, like a unified force in addressing and dealing with the fears that kept them from telling each other the truth about how they felt about one another—and how it scared them.

When first looking through a window of opportunity, it may feel like looking at death. But the couple deciding to face these unknown feelings for one another are, for the first time, putting their relationship on the path to true intimacy.

No More Excuses

Those of us affected by irrelationship, with or without being aware of it, often use an "until" strategy to sustain our approach to life—including caretaking of others. For example, we might say the following phrases.

- "Okay, I'll take care of you until . . ."
- "Until you can support yourself, I'll . . ."
- "I'll pay all the household expenses until . . ."

But the truth is that the longer we use the "untils," the more trapped we become by feelings of guilt and shame and brainlocked into obligations we never wanted. But, love is metaphorically and neurochemically blind. In such cases as these, passion early in the development of irrelationship can blind us to our own insecurities and deceive us into snap judgments about others that corner us into untenable situations. And we will stay with someone until these "untils" become threatening. Meanwhile, until never comes. Or, if it does, we bail rather than sticking around for the sequel and immediately start looking for the next "until-based" fantasy of saving or fixing.

Self-sufficiency has been well described in Alcoholics Anonymous' *Twelve Steps and Twelve Traditions*:

> The philosophy of self-sufficiency is not paying off. Plainly enough, it is a bone-crushing juggernaut whose final achievement is ruin. . . . Each of us had his own near-fatal encounter with the juggernaut of self-will, and has suffered enough under its weight to be willing to look for something better.[2]

The kind of "untils" that are really problematic to our recovery are the ones lurking under the fantasy of self-sufficiency, such as the following statements:

- "Sure, I'll let you help me *until* I'm back on my feet and working again.
- "Yes, I can acknowledge that I need you *until* I find someone else."
- "I can and will share my innermost thoughts with you *until* you betray me in some way.

Most of the "untils" suggest that we will go along with a change in routine until we either find a new process through which we can turn back to our ingrained habit of self-sufficiency; or prove that, although we gave it our best shot, it was always other people who let us down. Therefore, we don't dare take the risk of allowing anyone to take care of us.

The new process is really another version of the old dynamic in our irrelationship role of using others to sustain self-sufficiency, with the irrelationship payoff of defending against anxiety. The missing pieces are any idea of doing the work and any sense of self-knowledge. Both are laced with overwhelming anxiety that has long been brushed under the rug.

From within brainlock, irrelationship can generate elaborate systems of fantasy that sometimes overlap and reinforce each other. These include inflated conceptions of the rewards people deserve for their caregiving, which plays into the repetitive disappointment and righteousness that accompanies victimhood. Despite all this, sometimes an "until" allows a window of opportunity for seeing through a song-and-dance routine.

Ed and Jinny Find a Way Out

"I worked so hard and put in so much effort and look what it got me," said Ed to his girlfriend, Jinny. Ed was an executive at a major industrial company and had, in his words, worked his "tail off." He was also one of those people who told their grandchildren stories, like "When I was your age, I had to walk fifteen miles uphill through the snow to school and back home," to convey a sense of morals and values organized around hard work and extreme self-sacrifice.

Jinny had scheduled a consultation for couples' therapy. She believed that Ed needed treatment because he was smoking and drinking himself to death. She also found she had lost her tolerance for dealing with their irrelationship. Her grip on being a good Audience had been slipping as Ed's usual Performer role was unraveling, and she found herself forced to take over. As she did so, her feelings started to surface. Trouble? Good news, actually: it hinted that a window of opportunity was about to open.

They started out with a "bang," Jinny recalled. "Two elderly people who had lost their spouses and were whooping it up together in the big city." They drank; they smoked; and they carried on "just like two teenagers."

The dark cloud that undergirded these good times was Ed's terrible heartache and sense of being betrayed by some vague force termed "the universe" when his wife, Mickey, died. Ed believed wholeheartedly that he had worked his whole life for "heaven," which he called retirement. He and his wife struggled, saved, and raised two boys, and just prior to Ed's reward (retirement), Mickey was diagnosed with cancer and died within the year.

"I feel as if I lost Mickey before I was even able to appreciate her and could let her know I loved her and that everything I was doing—for my entire life it seemed—was for her and the boys. Amazing, I am not sure that anyone even knows that," Ed confessed. Left alone, his drinking and smoking progressed well beyond his ability to do anything but succumb to thinking that the only reward for all his hard work would be death.

His relationship with Jinny put a little stopgap in that process for a short while, but soon the tables had turned, and he was—for once in his life—the patient (the Audience) and not the selfless one who sacrificed. He was none too happy about that and was having trouble making sense of what happened and how he felt. Being dependent and helpless was not the reward Ed had in mind for all of his hard work as a veteran Performer in irrelationship.

Although Jinny's history was such that she gravitated toward being the Audience, in this round of the tug-o-war for being the dominant caregiver, Jinny was now the obvious Performer. But it was a victory she couldn't relish; she was much happier being the Audience. Yet here they were. Therapy was challenging their pattern and put an obvious strain on their silent brainlock by placing them in the opposite roles. A chink in the armor was appearing.

Understanding his struggle, what it was, what it represented, and what he would need to do to actually recover from his life-long position as a desperate and lonely Performer was the only thing which would save Ed's life. A caretaking role combined with an expectation for being rewarded for all that hard work can charge a deadly price and be a powerful force of resistance for actually living life fully.

The routines of Jinny and Ed—who started out mindlessly repeating their irrelationship roles from the past—were scrambled beyond repair, which turned out to be good news. The tumult of having their roles reversed allowed for them to see how one-sided, lop-sided, and isolating their previous roles had been. This insight provided a clear window of opportunity for Jinny and Ed to create a real relationship that worked against the feeling that each was completely alone.

For Ed and Jinny, their window of opportunity and the path to recovery felt both threatening and life-saving. Yet they took a deep breath and walked into a new territory that both could inhabit.

Toward Positive Change

Think about what might happen if you were able to put an end to your song-and-dance routine. Reflect and make notes using the following questions.

1. What will my relationship look like without our routines? What will I look like without my routine?

2. How will it feel as our relationship becomes mutually caring? Will it lead to discomfort? Arguments? A desire to leave?

3. What windows of opportunity have I noticed that would bring our song-and-dance routines to a halt? How did I react?

4. What would I need to know and feel to take advantage of a window of opportunity?

Part Four

Raising the Curtain on Recovery

From Irrelationship to Real Relationship

Chapter 9
A Brand New World

Congratulations! At last, you have made it to recovery. It's time to dismantle your irrelationship trap so you can establish new connections and ways of being based on openness and generosity of heart, rather than solely on the need to feel safe. You will begin to learn and practice ways to shift your mindset and reframe the patterns of brainlock. This will allow relational strategies based on healthier emotional states to become part of your playbook.

Stepping back from old habits of thought and behavior can be scary. But the mere *desire* to step back, bolstered with awareness of what's going on and what's at stake, makes conscious retooling possible and feasible. Caring relationships with others will develop from a more stable place at a more steady and gradual pace. Using the tools and examples of how people like you took action to find their way out of irrelationship, you will discover a way of life that meets your true needs and those of others.

After you identify your irrelationship role and its effects on your life, the next task is to develop a new basis for self-esteem and personal security. The primary goal of recovery is not to focus excessively on questions, such as "How did I come to choose irrelationship?", but to figure out how to live as a whole person without irrelationship.

You already know your childhood history and its markers corresponding to the GRAFTS formula from Chapter 4. Now it's time to design a course for your future.

Before beginning, remind yourself that the process of recovery isn't just about you; irrelationship is a reaction to the world, designed in the image and likeness of your earliest caregiving tactics directed at your childhood caregiver so that you could feel safe.

Recovery involves a lot of letting go of old ideas about emotional security, self-sufficiency, and isolation. This isn't easy of course, but the rewards are plentiful. It may help to remember that these habits are patterned as fear-based conditioning in the ventral pathways of the brain (recall that the ventral pathways are evolutionarily more ancient and automatic, while the dorsal pathways are more modern and associated with flexible learning, including the ventral striatum) which are the site of self-protective disaster plans that are activated at the first sign of danger. In irrelationship, these network patterns stay at play without much regard to what is actually happening. Stepping back, reflecting, thinking through feelings carefully and without unnecessary urgency, and building greater skills of self-awareness are a few of the ways you'll build change. This will be reflected as increased activity in the dorsal pathways, including the sites of language, executive function, and context-sensitive emotional regulation. This is the path to rewiring maladaptive patterns, thus changing behavioral tendencies in relationships and making the brain, and you, more flexible and adaptable in relation to yourself and others.

If this sounds complicated, don't worry. Your brain will follow your lead automatically.

Essential Tools for Recovery

Before we get into the five steps that will lead you out of your irrelationship, developing awareness of the importance of reciprocity is crucial. *Reciprocity* is the key that allows the prison break of recovery. It is the foundation for emotional and relational health and well-being, in other words, social support.

Experiencing *social support*, in turn, is associated with empowerment and psychological resilience,[1] and resilient people are empowered to see more alternatives, improving their potential to make better choices. For example, resilient people are more likely to view a breakup as an opportunity to learn and use that opportunity for more social and constructive activities at the same time they are grieving. They are *less* likely to return immediately to the dating scene, spend evenings getting drunk, look for random sex, or jump quickly into a new, ill-considered relationship. Reciprocity means co-creating with a partner or other close person a two-party, mutual relationship in which you begin to practice a new style of give-and-take that allows caring to flow to depths previously unexplored. Reciprocity is the vehicle by which emotional risk and investment, empathy, and intimacy become players in our relationships.

Brainlock reinforces the delusion that the relationship pattern we use to protect ourselves is a real relationship. So, how do you learn to relinquish control, tell the truth about yourself, and let the cards fall where they may?

Part of this answer involves learning to listen to and be present for your partner. Another part is learning to practice meeting in the middle, or the Self-Other Assessment, to create a safe space for self-disclosure—which will be explored in some depth later.

The Credit-Blame Syndrome

Irrelationship usually includes a lot of finger pointing, spoken and unspoken. You may be tempted to turn the tables for a moment and get a good look at how you've been shaking down and ripping off those closest to you. But dismantling irrelationship isn't about figuring out where to place blame; it's about analyzing your life-strategy to date so it can be taken apart and replaced.

Q: When am I not in irrelationship mode?

A: When what I am giving feels equal to what I am receiving in a relationship. This shows that my partner and I are on an equal footing in terms of reciprocity, mutuality, and collaboration.

It is easy to see what a rip-off it is to take all the credit for what's right about a relationship, but it is more difficult to see how we rip-off each other when we take responsibility for everything that is wrong. We're wired to ignore the real issues because these issues are what had to be hidden when these patterns and habits formed as children. We might think that anyone who considers him- or herself to be the caretaker in a relationship is the one who takes approximately 100 percent of the credit for what is right in a relationship and 0 percent of the blame for what is wrong. But when you consider that people who are Performers and Audiences in irrelationship have an impossible job of making others happy, it becomes more questionable that they would be any less stingy with the blame for what is wrong than they usually are with the credit for what is right.

Now, that might not be what it looks like on the surface. How many times does the Performer cry out, "No one appreciates me," "No one cares," "Everyone hates me," or "You don't understand" while the Audience feels the same but mostly grumbles and aches in isolation? We all feel like complaining when we aren't recognized for our goodness or when we feel like we are being short-changed. When taking on such impossible tasks, people in irrelationship set up themselves to take the brunt of the blaming. By promising to fix everything which cannot be fixed, the Performer takes on a leadership position—setting up the Performer to be the fall guy.

How can you move past the credit-blame trap, which is a big part of brainlock? The 40-20-40 Model can be used as a Self-Other Assessment that will give you the framework to break the pattern and make a difference.

Meeting in the Middle: Using the
40-20-40 Model as a Self-Other Assessment

In irrelationship, assigning credit and blame is easy. It is easy to take one-hundred percent credit for what's going right and place one-hundred percent blame for what's going wrong on your partner without even talking about it. Cognitive psychologists call this *black-and-white thinking*, resulting from a chronic state of threat. The anxiety of continually feeling threatened clouds the brain's higher functioning, leaving decision-making to older, more primitive parts of the brain. In this situation, agreeing to negotiation, or meeting in the middle, is difficult and subtle.

Try this experiment: Imagine that you and your partner are sitting in chairs ten feet apart. Imagine a line in the exact midpoint between both of you—a 50 percent line. That leaves five feet between each of you and the middle.

The 100% Model

You	Mid-Point	Me
0 Feet	5 Feet	10 Feet
0%	50%	100%

Now expand the width of the line in the middle to occupy twenty percent of the space between you. To do this you have to give up ten percent on each side—ten percent off your territory and ten percent off your partner's territory.

The 40-20-40 Model of Relationship

You		Expanded Middle		Me
0 Feet	4 Feet		6 Feet	10 Feet
	40%	20%	40%	

The 40-20-40 Model helps us to imagine what a reciprocal dynamic might look like on paper. Irrelationship does not accommodate this model. If each side were simply being asked to split responsibility for what goes right and what goes wrong in the relationship, the task would be relatively easy. However, a variety of factors are typically involved in every event and outcome. For example, the contributing factors to an automobile accident may include the automobile design and rigor of manufacturing practice; quality control; road condition; weather; and various factors associated with the driver and passengers. Given such complexity, assigning blame for an accident is no simple task. The usual methods used for assigning responsibility are liable to be too simple, both in analysis and in assigning blame.

Assigning responsibility for adverse events in a relationship is even more complicated because it involves not only individual characteristics and background but also the interplay of those factors in a relationship. In addition, every relationship has a personality, or dynamic, all its own— just as a couple's child does. To put it another way, the whole is more complicated than the sum of its parts.

In the case of a relationship, each party examines what he or she brings to the table and the effect it has on his or her partner. The 40-20-40 Model operates as a Self-Other Assessment (SOA).[2] It allows both people involved in an issue, conflict, or problem to pause and consider each one's own contribution—good and bad—to the issue at hand. Each member takes no more than 60 percent and no less than 40 percent responsibility (we can use the terms "credit" and "blame") for the issue at hand.

If we analyze that interchange using the 40-20-40 Model, we find the following: a willingness to accept—right at the beginning—40 percent accountability per partner with a 20 percent space to meet in the middle, negotiating and compromising on how much one partner might be invading or encroaching on the others space beyond 60 percent, while the other typically retreats behind the 40 percent contribution line. Using the 40-20-40 Model is a way of putting boundaries on caregiving contributions that allows a Performer to limit contributions (no more than 60 percent) and an Audience to extend contributions (no less than 40 percent) in the relationship.

Dinner and the Blame Game

Consider the following example: a couple orders dinner at a restaurant, but when the dinner is brought, mistakes have been made with the order. Countless times, the couple has encountered this type of mistake and fought about it. If it isn't about the food, it becomes something along the lines of:

- "You *always* confuse the waiter when you order."
- "Me? You can *never* make up your mind about what you want, and this is *always* the result."

In addition to the previous angry statements, the restaurant sometimes *does* make errors—even brings the wrong order to the table. But the real signal that something's wrong is how the words, "always" and "never" get thrown around. When that happens, something else is going on that hasn't been addressed—probably for a long time—between the two people. That something else is usually brainlock. In addition to not solving the immediate problem, it leaves each participant with physical symptoms— tension, stomach discomfort, changes in breathing pattern, and a feeling that he or she has "done it again."

Taking a Self-Other Assessment as a timeout helps us perform a spot-check inventory to see how each person has inadvertently contributed to the building conflict about something that might not need to be a big deal at all. The Self-Other Assessment can provide a moment for us to pause to ask ourselves, "How important is it (the issue, the problem, or the conflict) anyway?" That pause can provide us with an opportunity to pick our battles.

Think about how this situation looks in your life. If an issue is important and feels like a battle you need to engage in—and helps you better understand yourself and your relationship—then be objective when assessing what happened during a tense moment and see if you can understand why it happened. Divide responsibility for good or bad results proportionally between contributors, based on how their actions or inactions affected the result. Also, aside from the specifics of a particular argument, consider how accustomed ways of speaking and interacting contributed to the outcome.

If you start with a polarized, guilty-innocent model, remember that this rarely accounts for what's actually going on in a disagreement. In most cases, significant, underlying issues go unrecognized and unaccounted. Also, the common practice of scapegoating confuses the situation further, reducing the chance of figuring out what's really going on.

We already know how ripped off we feel when something doesn't go the way we want. What we usually don't see—or believe, even when it is stated clearly—is how we are ripping off our partners. Living inside of our own blind spots, we feel we must protect ourselves. We think we're shouldering the burden of the relationship and deserve a pat on the back for it, but what we're usually doing is invading our partner's territory and not accepting his or her contributions as valid (and devaluing them by doing so). In fact, we're denying our partner the opportunity to contribute meaningfully to our relationship, which keeps the relationship from blossoming into mutual, respectful love. Using the Self-Other Assessment, which includes the 40-20-40 Model, couples can create and participate more fully with genuine reciprocity. Each member allows the other the opportunity to advance and claim space and usefulness in the relationship—no less than 40 percent and no more than 60 percent. Barricades are surrendered, making way for caring and accountability.

The shared space becomes a way to meet in the middle—a co-created and maintained space for shared ownership of whatever happens between partners. The alternative is for both partners to remain isolated.

The Self-Other Assessment is a technique for reimagining and recreating every relationship in our lives. It provides a system for us to examine and then leave behind our irrelationship habits (which, like instincts, balk at investigation) so we can accept and face the challenges of true caring, meaningful relating, and building something genuine and enduring together. It also gives us a map for getting back on track when bad, old habits steer us the wrong way. The Self-Other Assessment creates a safe place to experiment with accepting and being accepted by others in a way that we have long feared would jeopardize our safety.

The primary tool for learning how to break out of irrelationship is the Self-Other Assessment. How the model works is explored in detail in the following chapters.

Toward Positive Change

The purpose of the following exercises is to teach us to recognize how we balance credit and blame in relationship. We learn to cultivate a greater degree of objectivity through the Self-Other Assessment. Learning to accept what another person has to offer is a foundation for overcoming isolation.

1. In what ways do you take 100 percent of the credit or blame for what happens in your relationships?

2. How is this part of your song-and-dance routine? How does the routine rob others in your life of their value? How does it protect you from people who you think you are close to?

3. Think about a situation from your life in which the Self-Other Assessment would be, or would have been, helpful. How could the Self-Other Assessment change your connection with a loved one?

4. In what ways might your life be enriched if you could allow yourself to live a life with no guarantees of how particular interactions or relationships would turn out?

5. Thinking about what you've read so far, which ideas make the prospect of changing your life exciting?

6. Does your reading make you think of particular people in your life with whom you'd like things to be different? Who are they and what would you like to change? What fears come up when you think of that possibility?

Chapter 10

The DREAM Sequence: Step-by-Step Recovery

Ultimately, recovering from irrelationship subverts the need for isolation by taking possession of how you think, feel, and act. The technique that breaks down our isolation is the DREAM Sequence. The most important tool of the technique is the Self-Other Assessment introduced in the previous chapter.

Either partner can call for a Self-Other Assessment any time or anywhere a problem or issue arises. This provides a structure and process for identifying what's happening with and between each party. Each party agrees—at least during the course of the meeting—to take no less than 40 percent and no more than 60 percent credit or blame for his or her part in the issue at hand (or, more generally, for the status of the relationship at the time).

The Self-Other Assessment allows us to observe and express the anxiety about intimacy, empathy, and emotional investment instead of acting it out to confirm our worst suspicions about other people. It allows for pause and leaves 20 percent of shared space to interact in a safe, flexible middle ground. Both people in the interaction are given a specified amount of time to discuss their contribution to the conflict, problem, or issue.

The following describes the basic structure and ground rules for a Self-Other Assessment.

- Both parties are expected to keep the focus on themselves, each sharing what she or he is feeling without fear of blame, criticism, or having it used against them.
- Each party must be able to safely acknowledge their part in what's happening, both good and bad.
- Both parties listen to *hear* what is being said without blame or criticism. This is vital for arriving at improved understanding of one another. *Placing blame or using shared information to manipulate the other is out of bounds.*
- Shares are strictly timed. Five minutes are suggested for each party's initial share and then three minutes for each share thereafter (with no interrupting or cross-talk), going back and forth until both parties feel they've achieved, or at least moved toward, resolution.

The effectiveness of this technique lies in each party's learning to feel free and safe stating what he or she needs to say with clarity and focus, without defensiveness, or without worrying about having to address unwelcome feedback or advice. Each party listens and learns *from* and *about* the other. With practice they become increasingly able to lay aside criticism and blame. Almost without realizing it, anxiety and old habits of defending oneself slip away, clearing a space for genuine caring for one another.

The DREAM Sequence teaches the skills needed to reverse brainlock and move from the rigidity of irrelationship into a space that allows for connection, spontaneity, and enjoyment of one another. But it literally goes deeper than that: these new emotional experiences actually create new neural pathways in the brain—pathways not created by anxiety and learning to live with anxiety.

Before beginning the DREAM Sequence, you'll need to start building a new conception of yourself that you can believe in, embrace, and use on the journey. The following list includes some points to think over and return to as you approach and work through the DREAM Sequence.

- Allow yourself a quiet time and place for the DREAM Sequence, always keeping in mind that the things you worry about don't have to be the loudest voice in your head.

- Remember that dreaming about the life you want is normal and part of being a healthy person.
- Remind yourself that the world will not fall apart if things seem not to go as you'd wanted or planned: the unknown or unpredictable doesn't have to be something to fear.

Research shows that athletes who imagine practicing their sport well actually do better when it comes time to play. Also, a study of animals' brain activity shows that when animals sleep, they practice what they have been learning.[1] People do the same thing; when awakened from sleep, people report dreaming of the same kind of activity they learned the day before. Take that as a cue for your approach to the DREAM Sequence.

Although visualization is a great tool, work is needed for new learning to settle in. So allow yourself to imagine and learn a new way of accepting and relating to yourself and to others as they *really are*.

The DREAM Sequence may feel foreign and even bizarre at first, but it's the beginning of breaking out of irrelationship. A deeply hidden part of yourself longs to get away from repeatedly choosing controlled and controlling relationships. Practicing an unconditionally accepting and loving relationship with yourself is the first step toward liberating the hidden you.

The DREAM Sequence

The DREAM Sequence is the nuts and bolts of recovery. DREAM is an acronym for Discovery, Repair, Empowerment, Alternatives, and Mutuality. These five steps are a practical technique for disentangling yourself from irrelationship. The steps may be worked sequentially, or they may be combined.

In the following chapters you'll find examples, stories, and techniques that will help you to understand and work each step.

The DREAM Sequence
Step 1 DISCOVERY
Hitting bottom and realizing that you're trapped in the song-and-dance routine of irrelationship. Allowing feelings of anxiety and isolation to break through the carefully constructed irrelationship defense system, which can be overwhelming. Beginning to learn what irrelationship is, and becoming willing to change. Becoming increasingly able to see how your song-and-dance routine has been a failure, and wanting to change how you have been living.
Step 2 REPAIR
Recognizing how irrelationship affects you as an individual. Overcoming natural resistance and repression and coming to understand and break out of dissociation. Engaging your partner in an interactive repair process. Understanding how your habit of hiding from connection with others can be changed. Coming to believe that you can safely accept what others have to offer—especially those closest to you. Leaning new ways of managing anxiety. Letting go of the idea that somebody has to be blamed.
Step 3 EMPOWERMENT
Gaining deeper self-understanding and acceptance. Identifying and describing your personal song-and-dance routine. Seeing how irrelationship keeps you from knowing *your* true self. Seeing how irrelationship prevents true relationships with others. Accepting accountability for your part—good and bad—in your relationships.

Step 4 ALTERNATIVES
Accepting the possibility that your thoughts and feelings about life and other people can be changed.
Implementing the Self-Other Assessment for managing anxiety, fear, anger, and conflict.
Beginning to see concrete examples of how your behavior can change and deliberately starting to change it.
Expanding your willingness and vision for change and growth.

Step 5 MUTUALITY
Embracing the vitality, unpredictability, and even the downsides of life as they really are.
Becoming increasingly open to and excited by the sharing of life in two-party relationships.
Allowing giving and receiving, including the "helping and being helped" part of reciprocity.
Living the 40-20-40 Model in sharing and accountability.
Continuing growth as individuals and as collaborators in relationships.

The DREAM Sequence is a technique for learning to give *and* receive in a relationship—it can be thought of as relationship sanity—and for developing the ability *to see and value* others. Over time, we see ourselves more honestly and create meaningful shifts out of irrelationship into real relationship. The DREAM Sequence awakens the capacity for co-creating partnerships and developing more secure attachment styles within more secure relationships. We learn new ways of managing anxiety that permit development of intimate relationships in which we can allow ourselves to feel vulnerable. We can even learn to feel protected *with and by* our partners, as opposed to being protected *from* our partners by our song-and-dance routines, which maintain insecure ways of relating. By working the DREAM Sequence, we unlearn the old survival techniques that produced brainlock and kept us apart from one another.

Each letter of the DREAM acronym includes a realization component (The Ah-ha), a function component (The How) and an action component (The Action), i.e., an exercise that includes inviting another person to join you in recovery. All of the steps encourage application of what you learn practicing the 40-20-40 Model, or meeting in the middle. The practice may be difficult and scary at first, but it gets easier with practice.

Step 1: Discovery
The Ah-ha

Accepting that something is wrong is the necessary platform for change. Self-improvement *requires* this acceptance, while resisting acceptance risks making things even worse. The first step in recovery is *discovering* your feelings and letting yourself be aware of them—the isolation, loneliness, anxiety, and fear that drove you to disappear from your emotions and choose to live in your hiding place. Although this part is usually uncomfortable, the acceptance of your true feelings is a window of opportunity. It can be compared to the hitting bottom that causes people with an addiction to seek help. Similarly, accepting the failure of your song-and-dance routine starts the process of moving toward a life of genuine relationships.

In Discovery, it can be relatively easy to understand and admit the ways that irrelationship developed and played out in your life and in your most significant relationships. In this stage, you identify the parts of the song-and-dance routine that you and your partner have jointly created and committed to, resulting in brainlock. You become able to see that a result of this defensive state is that you have been brushing up against the people closest to you without really touching them, which allows you to feel safe but only by isolating you. You also discover how you and your partner enact Performer or Audience roles to protect yourself from the relationship itself. This insight is the beginning of the journey toward freedom.

The How

The Self-Other Assessment is a pause for couples and people who are having problematic interactions with significant others. It can be even done with more than two people, say in a staff or departmental meeting. It's serves as a forum for taking inventory, making it a perfect space for extending Discovery.

Part of Discovery is *listening*, so if you are using a cell phone or ear buds, it's not going to work. Inner listening comes first. If you can't listen to yourself, you won't be able to listen anyone else. In the case of your irrelationship, you need to discover what your routine is saying to those around you, such as "Back off," "I'm fine," "I can help," or "I don't need you."

The 40-20-40 Model enforces *listening to understand* rather than listening to build up your defense and craft a rebuttal. This technique provides space for mindful, measured intentionality rather than erratic, anxiety-driven responses.

The Action

Discovery is hard work. Your task is to resist the pull of the familiar routine, and, instead, to create a new default for yourself and the significant people in your life. The following list explains your first set of actions.

1. Ask a person close to you to join you in Discovery.
2. Discuss the song-and-dance routine you share with that person. Look honestly and hard at your shared performances, both historically and currently.
3. Ask each other what you think of your performances—what were the benefits for each of you? What does this assessment tell you about yourselves and about what needs to be amended, fixed, or made better?

Step 2: Repair
The Ah-ha

The second step goes deeper as you explore and recognize the ways that being in irrelationship has affected you—especially by seeing through the self-repression and the isolation of brainlock. With recognition comes compassionate acceptance of yourself and insight into how you shut down awareness of anxiety. This clears space to see that the cost of distancing yourself from anxiety causes you to feel empty and distant from those around you. Facing and accepting alienated parts of yourself will probably require some hard and even frightening work. When you've identified ways you first started this process, you'll need to trace the threads back until you can identify what you didn't want to feel or know. The why may take longer, but it will come. As you examine these decisions, you'll begin to realize that they became unconscious habits.

If you can't remember enough to identify clearly what happened, examples in this book will help. Even if you can't remember what first made you deny your feelings, beginning this step will start reversing your unconscious suppression of them. In fact, deciding to look at what has been happening is the beginning of Repair.

Each act of Repair that you share with a significant other is, by definition, reciprocal, mutual, and complementary. This includes small misunderstandings and devastating blow-ups, including outside love affairs and violence. This process is called *interactive repair* and is a vital tool for moving forward into a healthy relationship.

If your "look-back" begins to feel as if it's faltering, that could be an indication that you're slipping back into isolation. To counteract this, increase your collaborative interactions with your partner. The most important ingredient is the *willingness to see the process through,* no matter how uneasy it makes you feel. Shared commitment to Repair allows acceptance and support to flow and keep you moving forward.

The How

Using the Self-Other Assessment—starting with each participant focusing on her- or himself—what she or he has said, done, felt, or feared in relation to her or his partner. The partner's task is to cultivate the practice of listening without demands, expectations, or faultfinding. Be vigilant in listening for things your partner says that disappoints expectations that she or he will fix you—or that you can and should fix her or him. Be open to discovering as partners that you are allies—not antagonists, not prisoners. Even if you disagree, you can agree that disagreeing is okay and normal and doesn't have to destroy your experience of being together.

One of the unexpected lessons to be learned is that *recovery depends on recognizing the failure of your song-and-dance routines.* Learning finally to call your failures by their proper names is essential to creating a new way of being with your partner.

As you step into this part of the process, be careful not to forget that Repair is interactive; you consciously use each incident of "getting it wrong" as an opportunity to begin to build new bonds of trust that would be unavailable without understanding how you failed. Learning how to get what's wrong back on track is how you build strength as a couple.

From the start, interactive repair is directed at crushing the delusion that healthy relationships can be built on one-directional caretaking. You learn instead to work through difficult issues jointly, putting aside your need to demonstrate who's more generous; who's more wounded; who's the rescuer; and who needs to be rescued. Repair *must* be interactive because you *require* others to see your own blind spots.

The viability of this type of process sharing can be seen in similar models, such as the client-therapist relationship and popular recovery programs. Willingness to commit to and stay with the process, no matter what, is the heart of Repair.

The Action

Implementing Repair can be done with your partner or some other significant person in your life. Ask that person to join you in exploring what it means to repair a close relationship.

1. Describe a conflict. Pay attention to details that, at first glance, may not seem important. If they come to mind, they probably *are* important.

2. Using the interactive repair process, analyze your part in the conflict. From an irrelationship perspective, the goal is either to resolve or begin resolving the problem in real time or for the person you're sitting with to help you formulate a repair plan for your relationship with someone else.

Step 3: Empowerment
The Ah-ha

Empowerment is relational. We are so thoroughly relational creatures that no one can realistically become empowered on one's own. It may not seem like it, but if you're following the DREAM Sequence, you are already implementing practices that are the building blocks of real relationships. If you stay with it, the process will change both how you see yourself and how you live in the real world.

With this change comes vulnerability. Yes, vulnerability—that thing you've been using irrelationship to hide from all along. While that's scary, especially at first, vulnerability builds empowerment because it creates emotional and mental flexibility that paradoxically strengthens your place in the world. A bonus is that as your posture toward the world changes, your brain will actually change to accommodate this better-integrated way of living. Parts of yourself that have been closed off from your conscious mind and from each other will begin to open up and share information. Without realizing it, you'll begin to accept and go with life as it is rather than being threatened or frightened by it. As this happens, you become able to accept what others have to offer from a place of discernment and self-determination. Your life will thrive, which it hasn't done in a long time—perhaps ever. Your world will become bigger and more comfortable as your capacity for empathy deepens.

Having said that, this part of the process is not without risky and scary parts; like an old demon whispering to you, the anxiety you'll undoubtedly feel, especially at first, will likely try to turn you back to familiar behaviors. And it will be tempting. But you already know the best answer for the allure of the old way: "I've done that scene, and I know how it plays out. Thanks, but no thanks."

The How

The five steps of the DREAM Sequence build on each other. One of their fundamental purposes is to create of a new vision of yourself who, free from old, self-stifling routines, lives in a give-and-take reliance on others. This is done by formulating actionable and specifically segmented goals that will show you how you're doing as you progress.

Begin by explicitly articulating specific aspects of past relationships that you want to change. Envision scenarios of contrasting behaviors. Nail down specific tasks and goals that would let you see what the change would actually look like; it may be something as simple as stepping back from a task you would ordinarily have insisted on doing yourself, perhaps at home or at work, to make sure it got done right. The stepping back can be accompanied by saying something, such as "I don't know if I'm in the best position to do this job" or "I don't think I'd be too good at this," thus opening the way for others to help. Or it could be the exact opposite; instead of deciding for others or assigning tasks, ask your partner, family member, or coworker for his or her ideas about how a task might be shared or completed.

Start with modest changes. Allow yourself to become accustomed to new styles of verbal or behavioral interactions. Try them with your partner, a coworker, or anyone you interact with. Afterward, review the interaction, thinking about how it felt while you were doing it, and how you feel about it now.

As you take on Empowerment, it is *important* to remind yourself as many times as you have to that no change is too small to make a difference; big changes are made of small pieces. Buying into these small pieces is actually creating healthy, new habits. You may also find it helpful to remind yourself that as soon as you start to make these seemingly small changes, your brain will literally start to build new pathways for them.

If it doesn't go well at first, step back and see if you can figure out why it's not working by asking yourself, *Am I shocking others by assuming a different attitude toward them? Are they waiting for me either to be the heavy lifter or to clean up after them?* Whatever it is, don't let it throw you. You're learning a new role for yourself that you and others will need a bit of time to get used to. Experimentation and fine-tuning are a natural part of the process. But almost immediately you will find that your communication with others will improve as your notion of yourself changes—and vice-versa.

By now, you may be getting a feeling that the isolation created by your stifling routines took away any genuine sense of personal integrity and power. Your contrived fables of self-sufficiency were, well, fables—delusions. Now you're moving into a different space with others and yourself.

Sharing the co-created space in the 40-20-40 Model is an almost concrete mutuality model for learning to allow others to be important to you without controlling them—to meet them as they really are with compassionate empathy. Compassionate empathy shares and accepts the feelings of another person without allowing the feelings to overwhelm, isolate, or control the fate of the relationship. Compassionate empathy allows unconditional acceptance of the other person and commitment to moving forward into a place of sharing and intimacy without fear. That's the *real* power in a *real* relationship.

The Action

Choose a companion for this step. It can be your partner, spouse, the person you worked with on the last phase, or someone else.

1. Delve more deeply into understanding the meaning, motivation, and mechanisms of your song-and-dance routine. What was it protecting you from and how did it do that?

2. Invite friends and others to brainstorm with you and identify strategies, examples, and techniques for creating mutually empowering relationships. This entails one of the paradoxical aspects of recovery: empowerment develops from learning to tolerate not having the answers or not being the solution. The action consists largely of becoming accustomed to saying, "I don't know." As comfort with not knowing and with admitting that you're afraid grows, so does acceptance.

3. Realizing that you don't have the solution doesn't translate into weakness; it's actually a marker of strength—empowerment. The more deeply and honestly you undertake this part of the process, the less it will feel like a risk and allow you to create more space for compassionate empathy and intimacy.

Step 4: Alternatives
The Ah-ha

Using what you've learned in the previous steps, you can now develop ways of interacting with the world that are not encumbered by the ways in which you have protected yourself from risk—investment—in your life and the lives of the significant people around you. Little by little, you become able to *show up* as the resourceful and talented person you really are. Oddly, your personal gifts may be as much a surprise to you as to others. You learned to keep your talents hidden to protect yourself from being hijacked into caretaking routines which you had no control. As indicated previously, you learned such adaptations as a small child when you were terrified that no one would be able to take care of you.

As you proceed, remind yourself that your old ways aren't something bad to be broken or ashamed of; old habits are an adaptation you learned out of perceived necessity. Now you can afford to reshape them with love and gentleness and without rebellion, recrimination, or fear of being ripped off. You're learning to occupy a new, more mindful place in the world that is compassionate to yourself and open to what others have to offer.

Your new self-understanding allows you to

- change how you see your life—past, present, and future;
- change how you perceive and connect with others;
- change your approach to and behavior in intimate relationships;
- explore the possibilities for growth and change in partnerships with others; and
- reform old habits into ways of being in the world that don't leave you with vague feelings of dissatisfaction, guilt, or resentment.

The How

Taking inventory is an integral part of the Self-Other Assessment. It is a means of implementing the 40-20-40 Model, or meeting in the middle. As the word "inventory" indicates, you take account of your deficits and assets—the parts you'd like to change and the parts you consider your strengths. This information is used to develop ways of interacting.

As you take inventory, give due credit for your strengths without becoming grandiose and avoid writing your deficits in such big letters that they're all you can see. Exaggeration in either direction gets in the way of a true understanding of yourself.

You can experiment with alternative perceptions of others and yourself and also with new behaviors to go with the perceptions as you take inventory. Try on and try out ways of being with others that aren't based on the fears you learned as a small child.

The Action

For this part of the process you will again need a trusted partner or companion. You can use either the person you've worked with on other phases of recovery or someone new with whom you feel comfortable.

1. Create a Self-Other Assessment or diagram of your assets and deficits. If you're doing the DREAM Sequence with a partner or spouse, this exercise should be performed together and may be discussed as you go, or discussion can be put off to a time that you're both comfortable talking about it. After all, this part is only the inventory—seeing what's there.

2. Try to be clear and explicit, using specific examples of your weaknesses, strengths, scary parts, and scared parts. The inventory may include experiences, reactions, and feelings that you don't understand, such as "I sometimes get frightened when I____" or "When I have to do_____ I want to _____." Even memories, pleasant or unpleasant, that arouse strong feelings about yourself will be useful, such as "When I have to _____, it reminds me of the time I _____ and scares the daylights out of me."

3. This phase calls on you, always, to listen carefully, treating your partner with the gentleness and respect with which you need your own inventory to be heard. Remember the purpose is not fault finding and criticism; its purpose is to practice hearing compassionately and without judgment.

4. Creating alternatives gently considers ways of disempowering deficits as well as fully appreciating assets. You and your partner should feel safe talking about both your traits. Consider ways that assets might be enlisted to counter deficits, both in yourself and in your partner.

Step 5: Mutuality
The Ah-ha

The Self-Other Assessment allows you to create and maintain mutuality with partners, family, coworkers, or anyone else. Thus far in the exercises, you've been bringing its underlying principles into play so that you become accustomed to how it works—its ground rules, purpose, and goals. As a model, it's the paradigm for Mutuality—the fifth step of the DREAM Sequence.

But old habits don't die from doing a series of exercises. The exercises are a technique for reducing the power of thought patterns that generated behaviors developed over a period of years. However, the decision to consider changing is the beginning of change, and the brain begins to record it immediately.

Probably the biggest task during recovery using the DREAM Sequence is surrendering to the idea that the cost of irrelationship outweighs the benefits. One reading of the book and the exercises isn't likely to settle that problem in your head. In fact, the idea of putting down your song-and-dance routine will probably make some alarms go off. But the idea that your life *just might* be different can be enough to make you commit and stick to it. Just remember that disarming your deep-seated defenses doesn't happen overnight, and old behaviors are probably going to resurface as they do for people recovering from addictions or abusive relationships. For the familiar to lose its hold takes time, and this includes the familiar ways you've related to others and used them to make yourself feel better. But the exercises in the DREAM Sequence are a practical way of cracking open bad, old habits and the thought patterns that underlie them.

As you continue to practice, your ability to expose yourself and practice *response prevention* will strengthen. You'll become more aware of underlying emotional states that prompt you to choose irrelationship. When you tolerate and learn from those emotional states, little by little, with increased self-exposure, you stop yourself from responding to those emotions in the entrenched old ways that haven't worked[2] and become better at being ready with a "no, thanks" response when an old habit begins to rear its ugly head. Practicing this immediately begins to clear a space for new habits—your brain begins creating pathways for them—and, ultimately, a space for the freedom, spontaneity, and unpredictability of life.

Paradoxically, this change, or the breaking out of brainlock, develops as you become increasingly good at keeping the focus on yourself—your assets and your feelings—and taking responsibility for where your fears take you when you become anxious, thus making it "all good"—provided you're telling yourself the truth about it. Change created this way works better than a full frontal assault of confrontation, criticism, and anger coming from yourself or others. Doing it this way is necessary to learning to practice collaboration and reciprocity, which are essentials of authentic relationships.

The How

Perhaps the best marker of a healthy relationship with oneself is the company one keeps. In other words, the people we keep around us—especially those with whom we are intimate—reveal the quality of love and openness in our lives.

Collaboration and reciprocity—mutuality or give-and-take—is the defining characteristic of intimacy. But it's also the defining characteristic of feeling as if you belong. What may be less obvious is that compassion is key; compassion reduces suffering by reducing isolation, but it is most effective when joined to carefully modulated empathy.

Now—speaking practically—how do you explore what your life looks like in terms of mutuality, intimacy, and compassion?

Again you use an inventory process similar to the one used to identify and assess your personal traits. In this case, however, you're profiling the characteristics of your *life* and your feelings about those characteristics, while keeping in mind the practice of sharing, reciprocity, and mutuality. As you go through this exercise, identify specific behaviors and actions you can take that are directed at acting your way into healthy thinking. This has the power to create healthier relationships—and not just romantic relationships—but every kind of relationship in your life.

An added value to abandoning the irrelationship trap is that it eliminates space for useless blame games. Instead, you cultivate the ability and desire to assume ownership of your relationships.

The Action

Meet again with the person who has been accompanying you through the process. Enumerate and discuss briefly the changes your work together has initiated.

1. What changes do each of you perceive?

2. What changes can you identify that affect each of you as individuals?

3. What changes have an impact on the dynamic between the two of you jointly? If you are working the DREAM Sequence with more than one person, these points should be discussed with each person individually.

4. Focusing on reciprocity, what changes do you see and feel in your willingness to benefit from what each other has to offer? Drawing out any change is useful, but try to address changes previously identified.

5. How did anxiety and need for security set the stage for your buying into irrelationship?

6. How did your ways of thinking and the choices you made become a setup for irrelationship?

7. Looking at the past, cite at least two examples that represent relationships based on the list of GRAFTS behaviors.

Before following Chris and Sally through the DREAM Sequence in the next chapter, consider Colette, a Performer, and Peter, a passive-aggressive Audience. Look at how they prepare for recovery by reimagining their lives. How does it feel to them to suggest changes in how they relate to others?

What are they afraid might or might not happen? Put yourself in their places as they start reimagining their lives. But remember that while much of this process is conscious and deliberate, intuition and unpredictability are constant players in human interaction.

A Good Self Is Hard to Find:
A Performer Reimagines Her Life

Like many Performers, Colette, had no clue how she used her song-and-dance routines. Beautiful, intelligent, and well educated, she couldn't figure out why she was still single. At thirty-eight years old, she was successful—even a bit of a work-a-holic—and believed that she was ready to settle down with the right guy and start a family.

Colette had read many popular self-help books about dating and finding the perfect partner and had memorized many rules about what to do and what not to do. Therapy had brought her to see the conflicts and ambivalence she felt about commitment. She tried online dating, which led no further than several short-term relationships that faded rapidly.

Colette didn't realize that she was deeply invested in a song-and-dance routine designed to deflect the possibility of falling in love. But she came by this strategy honestly. Like other Performers, Colette had fallen into the role of caregiver for a parent. Shortly after Colette was born, her mother, a lawyer, went back to work, leaving Colette at home with her depressed father, an unsuccessful artist. Before long, Colette had taken on the duty of cheering up her father.

After repeatedly failing to establish an intimate relationship with the men she dated, Colette began to wonder if something in her history was acting against her. Her decision to take a hard look at her history was the beginning of her going through the DREAM Sequence.

In Discovery, Colette reconnected with herself as a small child doing performance routines for her father, whose marriage and career had proven disappointing. Colette's ability alternatively to be good, right, funny, and smart—straight off the GRAFTS chart—were the only things that gave her father's life any validation and meaning.

When Colette moved into Repair she became able to recognize that her childhood song-and-dance routines essentially became her mating ritual and brought forward her old need to make her father happy into adulthood. Going further, Colette realized that her childhood routines diverted her attention from her unconscious perception that her mother and father were not happy together and were not interested in being parents.

This conflict ripened into a crisis as Colette got older. Her mother's distance from their home life led Colette to view her father almost as an orphan who had been abandoned by her mother and herself as trapped in a situation from which no escape was possible. The cold isolation of the situation was made worse by the indifference with which her mother and father treated one another.

As Colette continued in Repair, she was increasingly able to see that her approach to dating and the idea of intimacy was a repetition of old routines whose purpose was to ward off her anxiety at being left alone in a frightening world that she couldn't control. On the conscious level, Colette appeared to seek out men who, like her father, needed her to fix them. The reality, however, was different; she chose men who, unlike her father, resisted her insistent fixing routine and ultimately fled.

In the realm of psychological defense, Discovery, or recognition, is necessary for Repair; and Repair is the necessary precursor to the third step of the DREAM Sequence, Empowerment. Empowerment flows naturally and, for the most part, undramatically from the ability to articulate honestly one's own place in the confusion of irrelationship. It includes awareness, understanding and acceptance of where we've been and what we've been doing.

Awareness and conscious acknowledgement of her history and becoming able to see herself in action gave Colette the platform on which she was able to admit to herself that she hadn't been trying to date men at all. Instead, she was always on the lookout for a project—someone who needed cheering up and fixing. After she'd done what she needed to do to them, she then wanted them to go away. This was Colette's ah-ha moment.

When she was able to take a look at her pattern, it revealed another crucial fact of Colette's life: while the caretaking of her father had left her sad, hopeless, and worn out, it also taught Colette to keep herself inaccessible to men who may have been interested in her. By doing this, she protected herself from the possibility that she might again be cornered and punished by yet another man's intractable depression. In short, Colette's routine was to fix them and move them out. And to make sure she kept the routine going, Colette was attracted only to men who resisted fixing, or so she believed when she began dating them.

The ability to articulate her love-life strategy almost immediately allowed Colette to see options to it and enter the fourth step, Alternatives. Seeing that the fear-driven dissociative strategy she acted out with her father had ruined relationships with boyfriends made her want to get power over the unconscious strategy and end it.

Having become aware of how she had driven men away with her fix-it routine, Colette made the decision to learn to do things differently; she was ready for the final step, Mutuality. Although putting down her routine made her feel vulnerable and less ready and able to re-enter the dating arena, she was determined to try it.

Colette had plenty of personal qualities that attracted men's interest. When the word got around that she was ready to start dating again, the brother of one of her coworkers—a man whom she'd had a crush on years before—lost no time asking her for a date. This DREAM-driven coupling took Colette's life to a level she would never have been able to imagine, much less realize, unless she took the plunge and allowed a man to become a partner instead of a project.

Long-Distance Love: An Audience Reimagines His Life

Although a continent separated Peter from the extended family that he believed had rescued him when he was young, he still played the part of

Audience to them. He felt that he owed his business success to them and went to great lengths to show it.

Peter visited his home in the Caribbean several times a year. Even though he'd been living and working in the United States for over a decade, he didn't feel as if he'd ever transplanted. He insisted that his roots were still at home with his family, especially his aunt and uncle who owned a restaurant and were his primary caretakers. Peter believed they had taken him in because his mother and father didn't have time for him. Ultimately, Peter went to New York, moving in with his cousin, the daughter of the aunt and uncle.

Peter and his cousin started a restaurant of their own that did very well. However, no matter how hard Peter worked or how popular the restaurant became, he felt financially insecure. And even though he was sharing a home with his cousin, he was hounded by feelings of loneliness. At the same time, he was paradoxically unable to get past the feeling he had to prove himself to his aunt and uncle and show that he was appropriately grateful for all they had done for him.

This sounds like a rather sad story—and if it were true, it would be. But, the truth was that Peter's mother and father *did* care for him in every way they could. But with four children to support, both of them worked at least two jobs to keep the family afloat.

The popularity of the restaurant run by Peter's aunt and uncle caused him to idealize them. He felt privileged to have been rescued by them, when, in fact, they were allowing him to work long hours in the restaurant for very low wages even when he was a child. Peter, however, considering himself indebted to them, framed it differently, saying, "They taught me everything I know about the restaurant business." Finally realizing that no matter how hard he worked, nothing seemed to turn out right, Peter set out on the DREAM Sequence.

In the first step, Discovery, Peter started to see—after a lot of resistance— that his subservient idealization of his aunt and uncle was, in fact, a passive-aggressive battlefront directed at his parents in retaliation for their absence from his life. During his visits to the Caribbean, he took potshots at his mother and father while appearing to be a dutiful son. Even his role of admiring Audience for his aunt and uncle were equally calculated to punish his parents. In fact, the ultimate dig at them was he was successful in the business that his aunt and uncle had taught him.

Another new insight Peter developed was the ability to see that his aunt and uncle continued to view him as the young boy who they had actually exploited as a child. And even though he played Audience for his aunt and uncle, they didn't seem particularly engaged in performing for him. In fact, they hardly seemed interested in him at all.

Continuing to unpack what had gone on in his childhood years, Peter recognized that, while working long hours prevented him from seeing much of his mother and father, his ceaseless search for approval from the rest of his family reduced further his parents' opportunities for showing him the care and love he craved.

After a time, Peter could see that his mother and father had, perhaps naively, made what they believed was the best choice for the family. Unhappily, their desire to do the right thing exposed Peter's vulnerability and didn't meet his need to feel loved. When Peter turned this corner in Discovery, he let himself feel for first time that he needed and missed his parents. As a bonus, a place of empathy and caring opened up when he understood the sacrifices they had made and how painful their choices had been for them. He began to feel ashamed of the criticism and blame he'd heaped on them over the years.

His relationship with his family was not the only aspect of his life that Peter felt wasn't quite right. Although living in New York gave Peter the space to live as he liked, he studiously avoided romantic attachments. From the moment a man expressed interest in him, Peter let the prospective boyfriend know that he was too busy for a relationship. In this way, he avoided replays of the disappointment in love that his parents represented to him. On the flip side of this scenario, Peter made his uninterested cousin his business partner. He taught himself to idealize her in the same way he had with his aunt and uncle, even though, as an adult, she was no more interested in him than she was in the restaurant business. But her detachment was not a problem for Peter because a life built on irrelationship seeks safety by controlling the degree of attachment.

As new perspectives of himself and his family took root, Peter was increasingly desirous of putting anger and blame behind him. He actively sought, piece-by-piece, person by person, to put all the parts and relationships in his family in their proper place—including the aunt and uncle who hadn't treated him all that well when he was growing up. In other words, Peter had come to a perfect place for taking the next step in the DREAM Sequence.

As Peter entered Repair, it became increasingly clear that throughout his life he had deliberately guarded against disappointment in love by keeping himself unavailable. Realizing this behavior began with his mother and father, he knew the change had to start with them—the ball was in his court.

To begin with, Peter changed his priorities during his visits to the Caribbean. He wanted to know and love his parents, as he had never done. Of course, this took some time, spread over a number of visits—visits that included hours of conversation filled with sad and painful admissions on his part. But he was thrilled and fascinated to listen to his parents' stories about their lives before and after the birth of their children.

Repair began with Pete's willingness to change and tell and hear the truth about himself and his family. This action may sound simple, but for Peter it was powerful enough to change everything. Eagerness to change his life put Peter on the fast track through Repair and almost precipitously into the next step.

Peter was ready for Empowerment. He wanted not only to change in his life, but also he actively sought to rediscover and reground his relationship with his mother and father. At the same time, his need to make his aunt, uncle, and cousin feel that they were important to his success withered. Perhaps most significantly, the spite that had driven his visits to the Caribbean evaporated as he came to understand his mother and father's pain at being unable to reach their son.

Crucial to breaking out of irrelationship, Peter connected with his own pain while simultaneously understanding the years of pain his mother and father had lived with. This cleared space not only for empathizing with his parents but also for compassionately leading the way as the three of them built a new relationship.

Putting down the old ways of irrelationship made space for Peter to explore Alternatives with his family. Unexpectedly, Peter found that his apprehensions about falling in love were as ill founded as his anger toward his parents. Put another way, Peter's brainlock began to fall apart in this step. This opened the way for two major breakthroughs for Peter: he became proud of himself for the work he had done to make his restaurant a success instead of feeling driven to do it to mollify unresolved feelings toward his family, and he formed genuine friendships with people in his natural circle *and* began to enjoy dating interesting, eligible men.

Finally, space had been cleared for Mutuality. As Peter and his parents shared stories, years of bewildering estrangement gave way to feelings of genuine connection, love, and pride in one another. They were able to share together the pain and confusion about the past. Peter was able to tell his parents how that past had made him frightened of intimacy in his adult years, and they were able to accept this part of their son's life with some sadness but also with equanimity.

At the same time, an almost under-the-radar change developed between Peter and his aunt and uncle. A sensible, clear-eyed appreciation replaced his almost servile regard for them. This was a bit strange for all parties initially, but that relationship, too, settled into one that was mutually respectful.

Toward Positive Change

A purpose of the DREAM Sequence is to create a new image of your life *for yourself*. So be bold; nobody's going to ridicule you or hold you accountable for missed opportunities or misreading yourself or others. These guidelines can help you, but let your imagination take you wherever it will.

Part 1

1. Think about your song-and-dance routine.

   - When did your routine start? Do you remember why? What was going on with you and with the person closest to you at the time?

   - Can you see your routine as a way of taking care of someone else? Who was that person and how did you want to help him or her?

   - Do you remember doing the same routine at other times in your life for friends, coworkers, or others? What did the routine look like and how did it help them and you?

   - Has the same thing happened in romantic relationships? What did you have to offer that the other person needed?

2. Now think about what it was like when you began to feel that, in general, your life wasn't working.

   - What was happening and what were your thoughts and feelings at the time?

   - Did you connect those feelings with anything that had happened in the past? How did you respond?

3. You've already done some difficult work by looking at yourself. As a result of what you've been reading:

   - Can you describe changes in feelings toward others and toward your connection with them?

   - Are you able to connect changes in feelings with what you've learned about your song-and-dance routine?

Part 2

1. Try to imagine ways that your life could look different if you broke out of irrelationship with others and began to build real relationships.

2. Review the DREAM Sequence at the beginning of this chapter. As you consider each step, take note of the items that catch your attention and write about them. It is advised do this in several sittings; different points will probably jump out at you at different times, and you can always go back to it as you continue this exercise.

3. Look at your thoughts about yourself and about others that are suggested by the items in the DREAM Sequence table. In what areas can you see change, or, at least, a possibility of change? Keep in mind that changes that seem small may be more important than you realize.

4. How has your reading and this exercise changed how you see particular relationships? Relationships in general?

5. Finally, looking at the names of the five steps of the DREAM Sequence:

   - Identify specific, concrete behaviors you can start using in your life to make the changes you want.

   - Next to each new behavior, write fears or other issues that could get in the way of trying a new behavior.

   - Finally, think of things you could do or could remind yourself about that might help get past your fears.

Chapter 11

Living the Dream

No matter what you have lost or been unable to attain as a result of irrelationship, *needing* to escape won't be enough to make change; you have to *want* it. To be free of irrelationship, you need to have a clear-eyed, realistic relationship with the world.

While reading Chris and Sally's story, refer as needed to the DREAM Sequence chart in Chapter 10, on pages 154–155 for process clarification.

Step 1: Discovery

Sally and Chris accidentally stumbled into the DREAM Sequence without working with a therapist and without rigidly following the outline of the steps. This can happen easily if one or both parties identify a window of opportunity, and both are willing to share the risk of stepping through together.

Hanging around on a Sunday afternoon with his wife Sally, Chris came across an article in a popular magazine that said many couples go through long periods without sex. "Nice to feel normal all of a sudden," he said to Sally with just a hint of sarcasm.

Discovery happened—something was wrong—*really* wrong.

Without knowing what was happening, Chris and Sally were suddenly confronted with an unhappy reality about their relationship and a window of opportunity to change it. A moment before, they had scarcely a clue that they had been brainlocked in a safe irrelationship for most of their life together.

Many couples in supposedly intimate relationships are startled when a cursory examination of their sex life reveals that something is badly amiss. Counterintuitively, a serious sex-related issue isn't often the means of setting people on the road to Discovery; instead, ignoring the issue is one of the silently agreed upon conditions of their brainlock.

Much like the initial step of recognition and acceptance of a challenge that needs to be faced, Discovery in the DREAM Sequence entails realization and admission that something's wrong, which includes realizing that the problem affects most or all of a person's interactions. This is comparable to the impetus that causes people to seek psychotherapy, life coaching, meditation practice, twelve-step programs, and other strategies for personal growth.

At first Chris and Sally's discovery didn't seem particularly earth shattering or carry much insight into irrelationship. If asked, however, each would each have claimed to be the caretaker of the other while receiving little reciprocation. Chris's care of his wife and their children was not demonstrative, allowing Sally to believe she could rightly claim that she was the Performer to Chris's Audience role. The nature of irrelationship being what it is, their song-and-dance routine had gone unnoticed for years. For some reason, however, Chris's oblique reference to their non-sex life jarred both of them to change.

Step 2: Repair

Although neither Chris nor Sally consciously missed sex, they did miss the intimacy and sharing from the period when they first moved to New York and settled in a family-friendly neighborhood. Both were professionals happy in their jobs—Chris as a paramedic, Sally as a nurse. The arrival of two children rounded out a family portrait that looked right from the outside. True to the irrelationship model, however, it didn't feel particularly right to either of them—any more than it felt particularly wrong. In fact, it barely felt at all.

As mentioned, Chris was the partner who looked more like the Performer; he did most of the housework, including cooking and childcare. However, he increasingly felt separateness within their marriage that he interpreted as the result of sadness and disappointment on Sally's part about how their lives had turned out. Chris addressed his perception by going to great lengths to make Sally believe that her contributions to their life and family were the more vital. This was no easy task, considering that he did most of the housework and childcare. The easy-to-miss reality of their relationship was that, while Chris was actually the Performer, he deliberately chose to make himself the Audience to Sally's non-performance. In a sense, this was almost heroically unselfish on Chris's part. In reality, however, it did nothing to erase his awareness of the beneath-the-surface unhappiness in their life together.

Sally was the daughter of a couple who owned a successful small business in her hometown. A scandal involving her father and a staff member destroyed the business and her parents' marriage.

Sally came to the rescue. Taking on the role of Performer, she undertook to restore her family's standing in the community by becoming a prominent community volunteer and do-gooder. In addition, she ill-advisedly made herself the agent for saving her parents' marriage. Hoping to fix things, she conveyed messages back and forth across the battle lines, tweaking the messages in ways she hoped would make her mother and father more willing to be reconciled.

It backfired. When Sally's parents realized how she was manipulating them, they turned on her and began to use her as a scapegoat for *their* bad behavior. Ugly as this was, it exposed a darker level of dysfunction within the family. Sally's parenting her parents turned out to be part of an older pattern in which she tried to make right the distant, uninterested parenting she had received growing up. So to extract the care she needed from them as a child, Sally became her parents' caretaker. The long-term net result of casting herself as parent to her parents was that Sally ended up estranged from them. Believing with a child's credulousness that the world is—must be—fair and just, Sally held herself responsible for the disintegration of her family. When she went out into the world, she inevitably brought that burden of powerlessness and self-blame into her marriage.

Chris, the oldest of four children, was the son and grandson of accountants with a family-run tax preparation business in Baltimore, Maryland. After the store was vandalized repeatedly, the family pulled up stakes and moved to a small community in the Midwest.

Although leaving home and friends behind was difficult for Chris and his siblings, the change distressed his parents so much that any awareness of the children's needs was put aside. Bad feelings related to the move were so severe that they culminated in estrangement between Chris's parents and his paternal grandparents, who were part owners of the family business. The damage proved to be irreparable and left his parents deeply angry and resentful.

Chris's and Sally's family experiences had common threads. Both of them took on the role of caretakers in the midst of highly distressing periods in family life. Also they treated their distress by disappearing—Chris's elders essentially made him disappear from family life, and Sally actively "disappeared" her feelings about her family trauma.

For reasons that probably can't be explained, Sally and Chris were ready in that moment—when Chris read that magazine article and made the comment about their sex-life—to feel the loss of something they had created together in the past—a loss that had never been acknowledged or grieved. Not coincidentally, this was exactly how they had treated the lost connection with their families of origin—by pretending it hadn't happened or didn't matter.

When Chris found himself married to a woman who was unable to care for their children, he not only took on the roles of both parents, but he also went out of his way to make Sally feel better about her non-parenting by becoming the appreciative pseudo-Audience of Sally's pseudo-performance as a mother. This included Chris pretending to leave family care in Sally's hands, allowing her to believe that she was doing a great job of looking after the house and the kids. Ironically, Sally allowed Chris to believe the ruse was working for her, but she never escaped the nagging feeling that nothing she did was good enough.

Cases of sudden readiness for change in couples long locked down in irrelationship can occur. A relationship does not have to unravel quickly or suddenly crash and burn to indicate irrelationship or prompt change. Many people hiding from intimacy are not in tumultuous relationships but flat ones. So when the window of opportunity opens, don't delay taking the tools for Repair in hand; breakthrough is probably closer than you think.

That's how it was for Chris and Sally. Once they lowered defenses enough to start a conversation about where the sex had gone, they almost immediately remembered and reconnected with the "each other" who had excited them years before.

Step 3: Empowerment

In a flash after Chris made his gently mocking remark about their sex life, their marriage could have disappeared completely. When they looked into each other's eyes, Chris and Sally were startled to see someone distantly, but not coldly, remembered. In the next instant, both realized that they were conspiring to avoid exposing their individual and shared vulnerable places.

The time of crisis passed without either of them blinking. Instead, for the first time in a long time Chris and Sally's willingness to see one another came to the surface. Without either assent or argument, they began recovering the shared care and vulnerability toward each other long hidden by their song-and-dance routine.

This unplanned glimpse of one another turned the key to their locked-down desire to be together. Silently committing to the process, Sally and Chris breezed from Discovery to Repair and Empowerment. Each partner accepted that something had been seriously wrong and expressed a desire to make it right. By doing this, they immediately received and granted each other the right and place of Empowerment. Each partner could now see and accept the other's ineffectiveness in the relationship and reconsider the strengths and gifts each brought to their shared life. Perhaps most crucially, they were able to describe and accept the multisided Performer and Audience roles they had played for each other.

Telling the truth about their relationship made the terror underlying it dissolve on both sides, including the fear that their life together would go up in smoke if they knew the truth about each other. Before the conversation got very far, Sally suddenly grasped and articulated that her futile caretaking performance for Chris and the children was a futile attempt at amends for her failure to save her parents' marriage. In his concern for Sally, Chris then admitted that he had covered up his performance routines so that Sally would feel better about herself. But the truth was that, fearing that Sally would see him as a threat or a burden, Chris neutralized the risk by disappearing as much as he could.

As they named these troubling parts of their history, Chris and Sally ceased to be threatening. The high-alert signals attached to brainlock started to shut down, allowing each to listen empathetically to the other's story of fear and loneliness dating from before they met each other. They were easily able to see the connection between those stories and the story of their relationship—the initial thrill and excitement of being together, giving way to anxiety as they grew closer, and finally culminating in the song-and-dance routine they created to prevent their learning the truth about each other.

Chris and Sally's story highlights the power and subtlety of compassionate empathy as it neutralizes fear and empowers couples by allowing them to see themselves in one another.

Step 4: Alternatives

On that Sunday morning, Chris and Sally did not suddenly head to the bedroom, although they had made themselves naked to one another as they had never done—revealing to each other that they had been hidden, frightened souls. They were thrilled to realize that, having weathered many storms without falling apart, they could learn to collaborate to rebuild their life together.

Sharing honestly that day disclosed carefully guarded secrets they never had dared to reveal, but were now becoming the basis of their going forward together. As they talked about their song-and-dance routine, they playfully began making fun of their fear and rigidity. But the playfulness was the beginning of a deeper commitment to being together than they imagined possible.

Step 5: Mutuality

As they talked that morning, Sally said, "It's kind of funny how, when we wake up in the morning the program never seems to change."

"Yeah. It's been kind of like I'll show you mine if you show me yours—only nobody was really showing anybody anything," Chris replied.

This is how they started to say yes to their desire—their longing—for one another and became open to the thrill of what they didn't and couldn't know, namely, what would happen next. The unpredictable suddenly seemed a strangely inviting adventure *as long as they went through it together.*

Being able to allow your partner to inhabit your heart and your life brings about what is perhaps the biggest payoff of reciprocity. Offering yourself without fear of rejection and receiving without fear of being neutralized are markers of intimacy—true intimacy that doesn't overshadow independence or drain autonomy. Instead, it builds something completely new: a real relationship in which neither party feels alone and both parties want to care and nurture.

Looking back on their work through the DREAM Sequence, Chris and Sally wondered at how they took such pains to keep out of one another's way. The very things they avoided or suppressed were now a big part of what made their newly kindled love making so exciting. Truly enough, everyday fears and crises of real life were still a part—but only a part—of their lives. The difference today is that no matter what comes their way, Chris and Sally can *and* want to do it together.

Glen and Mai Let Their Love Open the Door

The next section features a couple introduced earlier in the book, Glen and Mai. The ending of Glen and Vicky's marriage was recounted in Chapter 2. Glen remained in therapy trying to work out how he had come to choose irrelationship. Some months after his divorce was finalized, he met a beautiful Japanese woman, Mai, whose story was told in Chapter 6. Their story includes a more detailed working of the DREAM Sequence.

At first, their relationship looked like a reprise of previous relationships. Mimicking his experience with Vicky, Glen claimed to have fallen in love within minutes of meeting Mai. He even described it as being "knocked in the head" just as he had been with Vicky.

Naturally, one wonders: How could a seasoned psychologist who'd spent so much time slashing his way through his defensive song-and-dance routine not have had a better handle on this? Putting his song-and-dance together with Mai's history would have tipped off any neutral observer that this was going to be—interesting.

The kickoff was when, after a few months, Mai moved into Glen's small apartment in Greenwich Village. He was still in analytic training, while Mai was working part-time as a caseworker for a social services agency in a different part of the city. They had a daughter shortly after they were married.

As noted elsewhere in this book, you can't outthink your feelings. Glen and Mai's adventure with the DREAM Sequence was a breakout not only from prison but also from solitary confinement. And during the breakout process, they didn't shy away from the use of explosive words and deeds.

Step 1: Discovery

When Glen and Mai began dating, Glen's unwillingness to allow Mai to default to the Audience role irritated her. She was highly invested in her fly-on-the-wall song-and-dance routine and resisted changing it. However, both she and Glen wanted to change the game—both of their games.

But the breakdown of a lifetime of fortified defenses didn't immediately clear the way for joy and celebration. Glen had learned enough from his first marriage to know that absence of friction was not a reliable marker of a good relationship. In fact, as developmental psychologists tell us, friction or failure is necessary for completing developmental tasks, including bonding. In other words, getting it wrong provides opportunity for learning to get it right, which is a vital process for couples building intimacy. Such sharing was painfully absent from Glen's previous marriage. In fact, his first wife disallowed even the suggestion that anything about their marriage might need fixing.

When the turmoil started in his marriage with Mai, Glen was able to frame it not only as a chance to process what seemed to be going wrong but also to develop tools for resolving relationship issues. Glen had come believe that this skill was essential to partnership between spouses.

Mai had learned her reluctance and reticence in this regard from her family of origin, where her primary role had been to attend quietly on her mother's denied pain. Glen's experience growing up was entirely different; his maternal grandmother was his primary support as a child, providing the nurturing that Glen's mother, barely out of her teens, wasn't prepared to provide. When his grandmother's husband died, concern for the young family's wellbeing led his grandmother to relocate closer to where Glen and his mother were living. Although Glen remained troubled and angry through childhood, his grandmother cared for him in ways that allowed him to feel safe enough to lower his defenses ever so slightly—enough for his grandmother's unconditional love to touch him. This experience proved crucial to Glen's ability in later life to trust himself to enter Discovery with Mai.

Tolerating Discovery was more complicated for Mai. By the time she arrived in the United States, she was nearly shattered. In social work school, she encountered others for the first time—professors, professionals, and peers—who valued her as a person and as a thinker. They provided her a glimpse of herself that was dramatically different from what she learned from her family. Nevertheless, her profound sense of being unlovable persisted. Her relationship with Glen not only challenged that view but even led her to wonder if devaluing herself was a ruse she used to avoid the risks involved in intimacy.

Step 2: Repair

Glen and Mai used the interactive repair process for the second step in the DREAM Sequence, which created a new foundation for their relationship. Reciprocity—in which each party learned to validate and value what the other offered—helped them reframe potential relationship disasters as opportunities for learning and growth. In time, both were able to objectify the old way of managing crises, i.e., by dissociation, so that this dysfunctional pattern became less powerful. Ultimately, this choice—and it was a *deliberate* choice—neutralized the power of crises that threatened the stability of their marriage.

But it didn't happen all at once. Glen and Mai had previously identified their places as Performer and Audience in irrelationship's deadlock and the brainlock that held it in place. But practice and, perhaps, setbacks were needed for them to learn how to find their way through conflicts. In one particularly rough episode, Mai became so angry with Glen that she packed a bag and took off for Japan with their daughter on a one-way ticket. Fortunately, Glen had learned enough by that time to know, within hours, he would have to follow Mai to her parents' home and humbly ask her to come back.

By the time they landed back in New York, Mai and Glen were clear that pretending they could simply walk away from their marriage was an idea that neither was interested in, no matter how angry they may get in any one moment, day, or week. They had to take the nuclear option off the table, and keep it off, or they would never be able to trust one another.

Mai and Glen went into couples' therapy with a practitioner who understood irrelationship and how to work through it. This decision was a vital step; their newfound willingness to work one day at a time as equals and allies was necessary for regrounding their marriage. This included learning to use the Self-Other Assessment, in which each person focuses on her- or himself, telling the truth about their feelings and fears, and takes responsibility for the impact that has on their family. Through this practice, Mai and Glen learned unconditional acceptance of what the other brought and offered, for better or for worse, to their relationship.

Learning this kind of teamwork involves honesty about oneself, discipline, and commitment to going forward, no matter what. Today Glen and Mai say with pride that the payoff has been beyond their wildest dreams of what a marriage *could* be.

Step 3: Empowerment

As Glen and Mai looked back at the work they'd done in Repair, they could see how dark their accustomed ways of treating problems and each other had been. But they could also see how letting their guard down, even a little, could have a subtle, positive effect on how they felt about each other. Opening the door of willingness slightly was enough to begin to let love in. This changed their whole idea of what love was and what it could do. Most dramatically, they could see—with no small amount of relief—old defenses and character flaws didn't have to destroy their marriage.

By stepping back from his Performer role, Glen allowed Mai to be a co-star in their relationship. Nothing like that ever happened in Glen's first marriage; his wife seemed content with a carefully circumscribed Audience role. By the time Glen met Mai, however, he knew that was not what he wanted anymore. And after reflecting on her history, Mai had lost her willingness to accept the part of inactive girlfriend. But this change was not going to be a easy.

Neither Glen nor Mai were experienced in the new roles they envisioned and how to make them fit together. But they were committed to *walking with* and *teaching and learning from* each other as they figured it out. This is the essence of compassionate empathy: the willingness to create a safe space for each other's feelings, needs, and fears. Paradoxically, practicing vulnerability and hospitality leads to Empowerment and a safe space for real relationship.

Step 4: Alternatives

People in irrelationship use it to hide not only their character flaws but also their assets from one another, and from themselves. When Glen refused to take up his familiar role as the Performer, he provided Mai with space that allowed her to see and take in the reality and meaning of her Audience role. As a result, hidden assets were allowed to surface, resulting in her becoming able to make different choices from those to which she was accustomed. Space was cleared for her—in fact for both of them—to permit new, open ways of being together. Naturally enough, they were cautious at first, but simply making a beginning initiated new feelings that drew both of them forward, which accelerated the willingness and process of change. Speaking in terms of the GRAFTS behaviors, Mai was discarding her "absent" act, while Glen was learning to put aside his "good" routine, i.e., obsessively trying to fix his wife without allowing her to contribute to his well-being.

Even in times of crisis, as when Mai precipitously fled to Japan, she was unable to deny that, angry as she felt on her way to the airport, she was powerless to separate her heart from Glen's. The love between them remains unchanged by whatever either was thinking or feeling at any one moment. While processing this experience, both could see, almost without realizing it, they had made a choice not to have their shared life destroyed by a traditional, dark sense of fate that Mai's grandmother cast over her family.

"I felt as though I had never been held," Mai told Glen one day as they were picking the brainlock each had brought to their marriage.

After a moment, Glen said, "I felt like I was caught in my mother's clenched fist."

This was the setup they needed to hold one another—but with a hand open to security and risk without having to fear being suffocated or discarded. This new, alternative mode of availability to one another powerfully advanced the healing they had needed for so long.

Step 5: Mutuality

Having opted out of the habits of the old days and deciding to see and seek Alternatives, Glen and Mai were free to design a life together on mutually agreed-upon terms.

Open dialogue and a longing to share as equal partners were aspects of the new territory Glen and Mai decided to stake out. In practical terms, they learned the 40-20-40 Model to create a shared-life space. Of the 100 percent whole, each claimed 40 percent for individuality and privacy while leaving 20 percent for unconditional sharing, dialogue, and exploration of what Mutuality would look and feel like.

The 40-20-40 Model is the staging area for compassionate empathy—sharing risk in the willingness to speak and hear without fear. The more profound and frightening the crisis managed with this technique is, the better the outlook for relationship survival and growth.

DREAM Sequence Practice:
The Setup for Compassionate Empathy

Try your hand at imagining a walkthrough of the DREAM Sequence. This practice is primarily intended for you to look at yourself and see how you relate to others. It may include reflections on someone else affecting your life who has a song-and-dance routine. That person may be a romantic partner, family member, friend, or someone else.

Beside each step, write corresponding ideas or short notations. Guidance is provided to help maintain focus on that particular step.

1. **Discovery:** Write down new insights or flashes about your behaviors or choices that have allowed you to maintain a safe distance from others.

How this might look: This could be acceptable social behaviors, such as not answering phone calls or avoiding eye contact, but it could be even subtler, such as missing questions or cues from people interested in you at a party or forgetting to respond to an email from someone.

2. **Repair:** Look at each of the behaviors identified in Discovery. For each one, imagine an alternative—a different behavior that could change the flow of an interaction. This new behavior may seem small, but even minor changes can open the way to major shifts in dealing with uneasy situations.

How this might look: You overhear a coworker who you sometimes talk with complaining about how she was treated by another coworker. Instead of walking the other way, you make eye contact, listen to what she says, nod, and then ask if she would like to have coffee later.

Important point to remember: You're not doing this to fix your coworker's situation; you're doing it to learn how to be available to another person.

3. **Empowerment:** Choose one of the distancing behaviors you've identified that you want to repair. Imagine ways that behavior may be changed in a close relationship or some other part of your life.

How this might look: You're having a meal with a partner, relative, or date who's describing a distressing situation from their workplace. Instead of giving advice on how to fix it, make eye contact and nod; but in your head step back. This is not to put distance between you but to provide space for him or her to finish describing the situation. When he or she pauses for your response, nod again to validate what was said. This practice isn't intended to signal agreement; its purpose is to let the person know that he or she is safe with you and doesn't have to wonder if you're going to argue or criticize.

Important point to remember: This practice isn't designed to make people think you're a nice person. Instead, you're learning to allow others to tell the truth about what's happening in their lives without being afraid of what you'll say.

4. **Alternatives:** In the previous step, you practiced accepting in silence a complaint or negative experience of someone you know. In Alternatives, learn techniques for *sharing* experience rather than buying into the Performer/Audience, or rescuer/ victim, model.

How this might look: After listening in silence to another person's negative experience, respond by sharing a similar experience of your own. Be careful not to present it as a criticism or to offer advice. As you relate your similar experience, focus on how you felt when it happened and when it was over. If your feelings were confused or took time to figure out, sharing that is important, too.

Important point to remember: Sharing similar experiences provides a chance to learn to listen to, *be in,* or *remember* painful experiences *with* another person. Its purpose isn't to give advice or tell the person what he or she should have done. Equally important, when talking about your experience, avoid language such as, "I know how you feel" as a way of railroading the conversation so that it becomes about you instead of about listening.

5. **Mutuality:** Practicing Mutuality as an individual takes a bit more imagination than practicing the previous steps. But, again, consciously practicing a new technique causes your brain to begin creating new, functional pathways for the behavior.

How this might look: Review the practice of sharing negative experiences in Empowerment and Alternatives. Bring your awareness to the silence that followed after the other person recounted her or his negative story.

- Recall and visualize your quiet nodding.

- Imagine the novelty of *not* offering advice or telling someone where he or she went wrong, regardless of how kindly you think you could do it.

- Imagine the quiet that ensues. This quiet is *acceptance.* It harbors no judgment and excludes anxiety and sullenness.

Now flip the script. The person who told you his or her story is now reciprocating your acceptance with acceptance. Even if you feel ashamed of your story, it's accepted with a silent, but engaged, compassionate nodding.

- Imagine the relief you feel when you realize that you're not going to be told that what you did was wrong or bad.

- Unexpectedly, you realize that failing to control a situation or badly mangling an interaction isn't going to bring the world down on your head. In fact, it doesn't even have to make you nervous.

Important point to remember: The purpose of this exercise is not to deny the significance or repercussions of your actions. Instead, it's a technique for learning how to share truths so they won't haunt you or your relationships. Losing your fear of being revealed makes it possible for you to be in authentic partnerships with others.

Chapter 12

Zoe and Victor Break Free

"I knew when I read the title of your blog that the time had come to contact you. Something about that word, *irrelationship*. And I knew—I just couldn't do it anymore," said Zoe when she called us.

Zoe first encountered the word "irrelationship" on our *Psychology Today* blog and wanted to know more. This is *me*—this is *us*, kept running through her mind. After a consultation, she started doing the DREAM Sequence with her husband Victor. Their experience impressively demonstrates how the DREAM Sequence can revolutionize a couple's life together.

"Our pet-names for each other were Ne'er-Do-Well and Shrew. Not promising for the long-term expectations of a marriage," Zoe reflected. At the time they started working with the DREAM Sequence, Zoe recently had her first child. As she reflected, Zoe said that she felt more as if this were her second child. Her well-educated husband had been unemployed for more than a year. Finding herself pregnant at such a time proved to be a crisis for both of them, or, in irrelationship terms, a window of opportunity.

Zoe and Victor met as undergraduates many years before. Although they had always been attracted to one another, they never succeeded in sustaining a connection. With each re-encounter and initial excitement, the connection would once again flame out. In telling their story, however, both maintained that when they reconnected, they once again felt a sense of familiarity—even a love-at-first-sight feeling. This went on for a decade.

After so many years of near misses, this pattern of approach-avoid began to read as failure; failure to connect or invite; failure to express interest; failure to make or let it happen; and failure to trust and love. Finally they succeeded in hobbling together a song-and-dance routine of irrelationship as a stand-in for actual intimacy.

They settled into a partnership that had the appearance of a shared life. Each had come by the ability to do this honestly. Zoe came from a family of serious academics. Her mother, father, and brother were full professors. Not sharing their interests, Zoe was effectively sidelined by her family, although she carefully concealed the impact this had on her. She was careful to reassure herself and her parents that she was fine, even taking up a cheerleading role for her parents, which she extended to her brother as he got older. Having internalized the message that she was less important in her family, she kept herself out of the way so that she didn't make demands that might interfere with the important work of her mother and father. She was even proud of how well she looked after herself growing up. However, almost from her first reading about irrelationship, Zoe knew that isolating herself as she had done not only denied herself the care she needed but also made her childhood and subsequent years terribly lonely.

Victor came by his childhood isolation and loneliness differently. He barely remembered his father, who left after his younger brother was born, requiring Victor to take up a caretaking role for his mother and brother. His Latina mother had immigrated to Connecticut with the handsome man who fathered Victor and abandoned them. As he matured, Victor realized how much his mother and brother depended on him. He described his mother as a beautiful, caring woman, but her dependence on him was made all the greater because of her never having quite adjusted to life in the United States. This experience in his formative years taught Victor to feel, as the man of the house, he must not need or ask for help—a trait he shared with Zoe.

However, when he met and finally married Zoe, this abruptly shifted. Since Victor had done all the caretaking as a child, he allowed himself the "luxury" of being in the role of the one who was looked after. For her part, Zoe was entirely ready, willing, and able to take the "looking after" part.

And so the song-and-dance routine began—and began to misfire early. The roles they had taken were a rebellious acting out against the poor parenting they received as children. Not surprisingly, they began to realize that what each was offering was *not* what the other wanted or needed. Each was entirely capable of caring for her- or himself, so what was being offered—or imposed—by the other became increasingly annoying. They began secretly to long for the days—years—when they had failed to connect, despite their obvious attraction to each other. Fortunately, the idea of failure figured prominently in their thoughts when Zoe and Victor—both well-educated professionals—looked at the DREAM Sequence questionnaire on the blog.

Step 1: Discovery

Zoe started, "We answered the questions from the *Psychology Today* website, and we knew that we were in trouble. *Do I keep trying to rescue the people I am drawn to?* Well, of course. But the shocking thing we discovered was that we *both* felt that way. What?"

Victor chimed in, "The next question was, *Do I keep hoping that they will fix or rescue me?* Neither one of us admitted that, but—later—we both admitted that this was a secret wish."

"Yes, that was a hard admission," Zoe added. "*Do I equate loving with taking care of?* Oh, GOD, Yes."

Victor nodded. "Yes."

"*Do I keep doing for my partner, even when I receive little in return?* Yes."

"No—not this time," said Victor. "But that was what I always did in the past."

"*Do my relationships feel more like work that play?*"

"Work!" they exclaimed simultaneously.

"*Do they enliven or exhaust me?*"

"Exhaust," they both replied.

"*Do they enrich my life?* Hah. What do you think?" replied Victor.

"I felt like a total failure. It felt like this was all on me," Zoe concluded.

One of Zoe and Victor's initial discoveries, which they came upon simultaneously, was that the years of failure had provided them with plenty of windows of opportunity to address their unspoken agreement. Probably the best example of this was when they flipped roles. Zoe became Victor's Performer-adviser, telling him how he could better himself—by getting a job—while Victor played Audience, pretending to be incompetent and needing Zoe's management skills.

Victor was surprised how easy it had been for him to put aside his old routine.

Victor: I gave up that old role without even knowing it. If you'd asked me, I'd have told you that taking care of Zoe and our daughter was like a fulltime job—since I didn't have one. Every day when I woke up, I would tell myself, even though I didn't have a job, I was more than making up for it with how much I put into our home-life.

Zoe: It was terrifying, sometimes nearly paralyzing to be in this caretaking role and unable to get any kind of caring response from Victor. And yet, at the same time, I told myself, *I don't need anyone to take care of me*; but it was strangely painful, and I had no idea why. It really played with my head that Victor was so passive about *everything*. And it hurt—it hurt my feelings and scared me. Somewhere down deep, I wondered if anyone was ever going to ask me if I needed or wanted anything. But it was more a feeling, resentment, rather than actual words. I knew I was pissed, and yet, I also knew—I thought I knew—that I didn't *want* anyone to think I needed him or her. It was so confusing.

About the time I started to realize I couldn't do it anymore, this Japanese band, Cibo Matto, came out with a song with a line in it that hit me—something about living in the place I wanted to live, but living there as a ghost. That spoke to me—the word, 'ghost.' I knew—I could remember what Victor was like all those years ago—and me, too—and I knew that's how we were living: as ghosts of ourselves.

Victor: I couldn't get it together, no matter how hard I tried, even though I sensed that if I didn't get a job and take on more responsibilities around the house, our relationship would just hit a wall and that would be the end. But at the same time, the idea of getting a job was worse—was even scarier.

Zoe: I made the initial contact for help. I happened to see the blog and wrote to the irrelationship group and told them how I was feeling. When they wrote back, I was surprised and relieved; they seemed to get it. They sent some communications guidelines for couples and some instructions on how to use them.

It was weird at first. It was all about making space so that both people could talk about what they wanted and what they were afraid of. Both of us had to learn to be honest about how we felt and be willing to listen to how our partner felt without interrupting. It's practicing the 40-20-40 Model. It gives you a way of talking and listening without interrupting.

The funny thing is that, when you're both doing it, things that you thought would make you mad or scared suddenly don't do that anymore. Or, not as much. Well, not right at first, maybe, but still, it helped us see that if we told the truth, that didn't mean everything was going to go down the drain. Anyway, after a while we became able to listen to each other without getting mad or running away. I think we were actually hearing each other for the first time since we'd known each other.

Step 2: Repair

Discovering the ways they had failed together was Victor and Zoe's window of opportunity for initiating Repair—which, like Discovery, is also interactive.

Zoe: It was hard to believe that my Performer role was a survival skill, an escape hatch from my loneliness. But the loneliness—that word "ghost" hit me pretty hard— loneliness was exactly what was waiting for me.

Victor: I just saw that taking care of my mother—my family—was something that someone had to do. No one else seemed to be capable of doing it. But I never thought I was doing it because I was scared.

Victor and Zoe had fortuitously found failure and were committed to changing—to using interactive repair and staying with it no matter what. After years of hiding from one another, this kind of commitment was new to both of them.

In the best of circumstances, interactive repair probably happens countless times each day when we are infants. Mothers, fathers, and other caretakers try to figure out what we need—take their best shot at figuring out what we try to communicate to them—and then do what they can to meet those needs—especially the need for safety.[1]

As adults, interactive repair occurs when we work actively with our partners to transition back to a positive emotional state without ignoring or denying our difficult emotional states. By doing interactive repair together, Zoe and Victor learned that negative emotions processed through the Self-Other Assessment could actually create greater closeness and intimacy. Put another way, using the DREAM Sequence provides a way of turning a failure into a new bond of intimacy built of reliability, trust, and support.

As a first step, Victor and Zoe were able to identify with what they learned about irrelationship.

Zoe: I was—I am—a hardcore Performer, while Victor is definitely the Audience. But both of us were helping the other to steer away from closeness and from investing in each other. Well, if we were doing that, what else was our song-and-dance routine doing?

Victor: Yeah. And it wasn't just about *our* relationship; we did it everywhere—during childhood, with friends, at work—and, of course, with old girlfriends and boyfriends.

Zoe: What was interesting was, as different as our routines were— are—it seemed that our triggers were very similar. We could both admit that the slightest hint of rejection or abandonment in *any* relationship would send us into a frenzied song-and-dance routine. We were able to really hear each other, and—as odd as it seemed at the time—to relate to each other. I remember feeling so sad about how Vic was treated.

Victor: I felt the same way about Zoe. It was so painful to think about her left all alone while the rest of her family was out conquering the world. After that, we followed the suggestion and made separate lists of positive ways to deal with anxiety. We felt silly but could laugh about it when we compared lists and found that both of us had put *talking to each other* as number one.

Zoe: The idea of brainlock tripped me up a bit. I always felt very psychologically minded, but I couldn't get around seeing the results of the unconscious agreements that Victor and I made to and with each other. As much as I wanted to get better, I still wanted to believe that pressing Victor to get a good job would fix him—and us. But now I see that brainlock—getting tied up in this thing together—proves that we had to *do* it together in the first place. It was quite a slap in the face.

Victor: It wasn't like that for me—a slap in the face—but it was definitely disconcerting. What really knocked me over was realizing that even though I thought everything I did, I did for Zoe, but the fact was that my letting Zoe be the power person in our home actually kept me from giving her what she really wanted and needed. That was hard to come to grips with—and telling her about it was even worse. But we had made deals with our parents, and we believed those deals had worked. So we bought into them—brainlock. That kept us safe—and distant—for a long time. It kept us from living together, and then, when we were finally living together, it kept us away from each other. If we hadn't found the DREAM

Sequence, I think we'd have kept doing whatever it took to keep out the other.

Zoe: It took time for the anxiety, the fear, to die down so I could just *say* what I needed to say without running. Luckily all along, I knew Victor was worth it to me. But sometimes it was still kind of a leap of faith to act as if I—we—could survive if I told him what I was really feeling. Before the DREAM Sequence, I knew I had to keep some of my feelings under wraps for me to survive and for Vic to stay with me. But somewhere in the literature it says something like, "You're an adult now. You can handle a lot more anxiety than you could when you started your routine as a kid."

As far as GRAFTS goes, at first I thought I was an "A" for absent; but when I really thought about it, there was no question that I was a "T" as in tense. I totally lived in a state of anxiety without knowing it. But everything I did was soaked in it.

As a caretaker, I was driven. I didn't just let my parents off the hook for being lousy parents; I took over their responsibilities. And not just for me but for my younger brother, too. Funny thing is he also went on to be a star academic like they all are. And, yes, I thought I was responsible for *that* also. I was totally unable to ask them for anything. But the same time, I was afraid that nothing I did would be good enough. As it turned out, of course, it didn't matter; they hardly noticed anything I did, and I got to a place where I made sure it stayed that way.

On the surface, Vic's and my routines look totally different. But the truth is, even though I sometimes lose it with Victor, afterward I'm terrified he's going to leave me. But it's even deeper; I have this belief that he'd be better off without me—that if he *did* leave, that would be *his* ticket to stardom.

Victor: That's funny, Zoe—but not in a ha-ha way. In the GRAFTS thing, I definitely believed I had to be "smart," though pretty often I'd use "funny" to break the tension in my family. It was so hard to live in that sometimes—I wished that my mom would kick me out of the house. Strange, huh? Considering how afraid I've always been of being abandoned? I kept up my routines, even though I wanted out—half-hoping something would make her kick me out of the house.

It seems as if that's the game I was playing with you [Zoe], although I think I also get a "T" for tense. I've always kind of walked on eggshells around you, so scared I was going to lose you. But I can see that the whole thing was a bizarre way of taking care of you. Both of us needed the other to be in the role we were in so that we could feel safe.

In this phase of the DREAM Sequence, Victor and Zoe were finding out that caring for another person isn't a one-way street: both parties participate with neither party setting the agenda—designing the solution—for the other. This is the essence of breaking brainlock and dissolving the song-and-dance routine. Nobody gets to be hero or victim, or to be righteous or rescued. Everybody plays, and everybody tells and listens for the truth about what they need.

Step 3: Empowerment

Zoe: Even though my routine made me look like the powerful one—the breadwinner who took care of Victor and Evie, our daughter, it actually sets me up to be the victim. I'd come home after working two jobs and find Victor goofing off on the computer, and the baby hadn't been fed or changed—and I'd go berserk. But it didn't feel like I was just attacking him; it was more like he was attacking me, and I was just returning fire. But I was so depressed and insecure that I didn't feel as if I had much more to offer than Victor did.

Victor: When the storm would die down, we'd return to business as usual. Except that I felt a little smaller each time—like I was a kid Zoe was looking after, just like Evie. It felt awful, but neither of us seemed about to talk about it once Zoe's anger had passed.

Meanwhile, I still told myself I didn't need anyone, but that just added to the conflict—to my conflict—because all my life I wanted somebody to take care of me. Meanwhile, Zoe hated me for not stepping up to the plate. You can't really blame her, but I hated her right back—not for getting mad at me but for mothering me. I really felt that was what she was doing, but it was making her a wreck.

Zoe: It's true. Only now I know that having a real grown-up, caring, and contributing partner would have scared me even more. That is why, instead of really supporting your trying to find your way, I kept kicking your feet out from under you.

Victor: And I was rubbing my not getting a job in your face even more by not doing things around the house I could have done—especially taking good care of our daughter.

Zoe and Victor were becoming increasingly able, despite pain and tears, to talk about what their relationship had been like. Both could see the part each had played in their song-and-dance routine. Becoming more honest increased Zoe and Victor's feeling of safety with one another, despite that the sharing even included revealing destructive behaviors toward themselves and one another. At times, this flipped into accusatory inventory taking with the clincher, "after all I do for you."

But they kept at it, guided by the principle of keeping the focus on oneself using the Self-Other Assessment. As they came to fear attack less, they lowered defenses and were less tempted to resort to the old song-and-dance routine. A moment came when, to their surprise, they realized they longed for and missed each other. For Zoe and Victor, this was Empowerment—an empowerment they could see and draw from together rather than parasitically, with one depleting the other.

Step 4: Alternatives

Zoe: The DREAM Sequence, which takes you to the stepping-off place for compassionate empathy, is how I realized that an alternative way of living with Victor wasn't just about different behavior; it's an alternative way of feeling, well actually, of *sharing* feelings. I'd had no clue I was burning myself out in the way I related to Victor. And not just Victor; I brought these ridiculous expectations with me to everybody and everywhere I went, including the punishing part. And it all went back to some twisted idea I had that I was putting myself in others' shoes and always doing for others and deserved to be rewarded for it.

Victor: And I stuck to my part. I knew that Zoe was suffering, but I couldn't bring myself to think about what her life was like and what it was costing her. Any time I caught a glimpse of it, either in her face or in my own head, I got nervous and turned away as fast as I could. It could almost make me panic.

Zoe: That's why, for me, it's been so important to understand how irrelationship defends against anxiety. I've been able to see—it's taken awhile, but, yeah, I'm getting it—our routines protect us from the fear that's attached to getting what we think we want. But it really doesn't work. It *doesn't* protect us from the stressors of real life—job, unemployment, money, or even our no-sex sex life. But it sure kept us away from each other.

Victor: How could we have a sex life? I was a kid trying to keep away from my overbearing mother. Looking at it now, it sure does look like we were committed to not being with each other—under the same roof. And now we know why. After what we both learned at home, why would we ever think we could trust being in love? Could we trust another person to show up for us? Yeah, we were attracted to each other, all right, but life had taught us that love was a delusion, and neither of us was about to risk it.

If you think about it, it's pretty quirky that we've ended up doing this work together. Without the DREAM Sequence, I think our desperation would finally have driven us out of the house. Instead—it still seems like a miracle—we're actually walking through this together—partners for the first time ever. But what I can't get over is that blame doesn't seem to have any part in it. The whole idea is just meaningless.

One day when we were doing the Self-Other Assessment, I suddenly felt this new compassion for Zoe. In a way, it was as if nothing I knew about her had made sense until that moment. And then—yikes—I could finally begin to understand what I had put her through.

A point came where the momentum completely changed. I got a job—and not just an okay job for the sake of providing income. It was with this great company, and *they* thought *I* was a great catch. Meanwhile, I'd been working on starting my own company using a business model I had developed, and I really didn't want to give that up. Although money was pouring in, I had to consider the possibility that the dream of having my own business was sabotaging my looking for a job and caring for my family. Still, this Victor is the Victor I'd always wanted Zoe to believe she had married. Not so much I was a rich guy, but that I could and would do what it takes to take care of my family.

It was scary, but what was the option? I was scared of the risk of being in love with Zoe, but I kept it at a distance, though I'd known something was wrong for a long time. Even after we started working on the DREAM Sequence, it was a while before I let in the idea that Zoe and I were supposed to be equals—*were* equals in our marriage. When Evie was born, the distance began to feel like a pain inside not just my head but in my body. After we got into the DREAM Sequence, I finally allowed myself to feel love for Zoe—and let her love me.

Zoe: For the first time ever, the DREAM Sequence got us talking about trust.

Victor: We had some confused ideas about trust. Like—I trusted Zoe, meaning I felt I had nothing good to offer her and trusted her to accept that and not expect anything more of me.

Zoe: Yeah, and I trusted Victor to keep himself locked up and unable or unwilling to give anything to our marriage. It was a stalemate. Or—I guess in irrelationship language that was a brainlock.

Victor: Yes, and it was painful and lonely. And it just drained any excitement in anything—stifling, just like it says about brainlock. Being unable to give or get—take your choice; it's awful both ways.

Zoe: It is kind of wacky that the more traditional version of trust was never really an issue for us. At the rock bottom place that we'd been, it seemed as if the typical trust stuff would have been better in a way because it would have provided us a way out.

Victor: Boy has that changed. Now we're learning to trust that we won't get scared—or scared enough to take off. Instead, we stick around to see what the makeup is going to be like after a rough spot.

Among the alternatives they explored, Zoe and Victor looked at new ways of walking through old tasks and routines so they could turn to new ways of sharing life, and not just within their marriage and home. They learned alternative ways of life outside their household. Previously isolated from one another in their marriage and home, they began reaching out to others, including couples they knew and liked but had never been close to. They were surprised at how much they enjoyed things that had so little savor when living in isolation from one another.

Step 5: Mutuality

Zoe: When we started the DREAM Sequence, I think the last thing I expected to end up with was what I had actually started out with. The next surprise was that I had never really lost it; I was just hiding from it. Turns out I was right the first time, though. A life with Victor was what I really wanted and could still have. I just had to let go of what I'd learned about being close to someone and let myself—no, let *us*—have one another.

In learning that giving and receiving wasn't a threat to their safety, Zoe and Victor were able to begin the practice of the final step, Mutuality. In the language of irrelationship, mutuality is the practice of each party's acceptance of what the other has to offer and opening the door to compassionate empathy.

Zoe: The way I understand it, compassionate empathy isn't just feeling empathy for each other's situation; it's also the willingness to walk together out of the dark places the past took us and left us. Both of us had bought into that dark place—they call it brainlock—but the willingness behind compassionate empathy takes brainlock apart. After that, the song-and-dance routine seems, well, just silly. Without the routine, we've been able to live in love with each other in a way we never did before.

Victor: No. I was really locked into the singing and dancing to keep from thinking about what my wife actually felt or was going through. Stopping the routine was not an option—was way too scary. But neither of us had a clue that was what our life was made of—a performance routine that kept us apart. At the same time, I hated myself for it—for not touching her, listening to her—not even asking. But I knew the whole time that it was messed up. A voice deep inside kept telling me to just *ask* her how she was doing. But I couldn't. I just couldn't.

Zoe: You know what's funny? When we started the DREAM Sequence, and I realized that we'd made the irrelationship together, I had this strange feeling of relief that I didn't understand right at first. And then, well, I started to get excited. Deep down, I felt I still loved you. And if both of us had stuck around to make our irrelationship [work] instead of just walking away, well, that meant that we *really did* care about each other. So if we could create irrelationship, then we could take it apart and make something else. I remember one day looking at Evie and thinking, *If Vic and I can make that beautiful little girl together—well, why not?*

Victor: I still can't believe what a job it was holding everything together. . . I feel so honored that you stuck around to do the work of pulling it apart with me.

Zoe: Isn't that the truth? I was always patting myself on the back for how hard I worked for my family. And the whole time I wasn't helping my family at all. It backfired, creating such a wall between us.

And there was Victor on the other side of that wall, doing his version the same thing, except he was pretending he couldn't do anything right, pretending to be incompetent so I'd could take credit for everything that was holding our life together. An image popped into my mind once of two blindfolded people in a tug-of-war. That's what it was like; we were fighting against each other without seeing what was happening to the other person. And, well, in a way it worked because I never even came close to thinking that this incompetent person had something to offer that could make me feel better.

As we went through the DREAM Sequence, it got us to imagine a life together in which we were who we wanted to be without being afraid of what would happen. At first it wasn't easy to think about the box we'd put ourselves in, but we kept at it. It was exciting but almost shocking. No—it really *was* shocking to be telling each other things we were sure would make him or her run away. Sometimes it was so unsettling I was sure that the next morning we would pretend it hadn't happened and go back to the old song-and-dance. But that never happened. As we stood aside from our roles and looked at them, it started to dawn on us that we had been keeping ourselves, and each other, in roles that were, well, like prison cells. And it was weird to realize—kind of disorienting—*Who am I then? Where is this going to end up?*

But what was even weirder was doing that part somehow got us back in touch with the person we had been crazy about when we first met. In a way, it was almost mundane: no fireworks, no grand and glorious dreams of what we wanted to do with each other. It was just—each other. But it was also like those late night conversations in the coffee shop that we didn't want to end. All we'd do was sit talking about, well, anything; it didn't matter what. And that was before we even started dating seriously.

Well, in a way, doing the DREAM Sequence has gotten us back in touch with ordinary excitement, except it's better now because the DREAM Sequence has taught us how to listen *for one another.* And we now know that, no matter what, we don't have to let anything destroy what we've found.

Through the DREAM Sequence, Zoe and Victor were now in a relationship—a real relationship—that not only tolerated but also actively sought compassionate empathy, intimacy, and emotional risk. This was the miracle. By using the DREAM Sequence, they found their greatest and most prized treasure: each other.

Toward Positive Change

1. Who, of the people we've followed through the DREAM Sequence—Colette, Peter, Sally, Chris, Glen, Mai, Zoe, or Victor—do you most relate to? Why?

2. Describe the transformation you see taking place in that person. How do you relate to her or his transformation?

3. How does—or would—this change affect any relationship in your life?

4. How is reading this book and exploring the DREAM Sequence affecting how you see yourself?

Toward Compassionate Empathy

Compassionate empathy is not a feeling for oneself or for another person; it's a shared process that brings us to the ability to see and accept the needs, fears, and humanity of ourselves and another person—or persons. Put another way, compassionate empathy is a technique for problem solving in relationships that's grounded in the deepest places of our humanity.

The DREAM Sequence culminates with Mutuality, which is the gateway to compassionate empathy. The following is an exercise based on the DREAM Sequence intended to bring you to a clearer understanding of the dynamics of compassionate empathy and how it fits in your everyday life and relationships. You'll need someone to work on this with you, asking one another the following questions. Be aware that the DREAM Sequence is a complex practice that will include steps backward as well as steps forward, which is a normal part of the process and should not be rushed. So give yourself as much time and as many sittings as **you** need to understand how you use irrelationship and how to take it apart.

Discovery

- When I meet new people, am I on the lookout for somebody new to fix or help? What does this look and sound like? How does it feel to say this in front of another person?

- Am I hoping to be fixed or rescued? What cues am I looking or listening for?

- Do I equate loving someone with taking care of him or her?

- Do I keep doing things for my partner or others, even when I don't get much in return?

Repair

Talk with each other about a relationship with someone that hasn't gone or isn't going the way you'd hoped.
- Based on the ideas in this book, do you recognize a pattern in how you interact with this person?
- Choose another person and discuss the similarities and differences you see in your interactions with that person.
- Identify areas of interaction with others in which you recognize brainlock.

- Identify behaviors that may be parts of a song-and-dance routine for yourself and your partner.

- Since you started looking at the DREAM Sequence, have you seen a change in your approach to others? How about in your approach to your partner? Be specific. Remember that little changes on the outside can mean big changes on the inside.

Empowerment

Think about the GRAFTS behaviors: *G*ood, *R*ight, *A*bsent, *F*unny, *T*ense, and *S*mart.

- Are you still using the GRAFTS behavior, or behaviors, you saw in yourself when you first read about GRAFTS? What GRAFTS behavior are you using on your partner?

- As you do this exercise, can you see anything you are deliberately trying to change? Remember that creating empowerment is a joint exercise. Can you see ways that you may be empowering one another right now?

- Think about the idea of compassion and how caring for others makes the two of you vulnerable to one another. To develop a safe space for each other, begin a Self-Other Assessment by describing what you feel is your contribution to what works and doesn't work in your relationship.

- Are you able to decide who is the Performer and who is the Audience? Tell one another what you think his or her role may feel like *without* judgment or criticism. Don't move to the next exercise until you've allowed plenty of time for each other's experience and perspective to sink in.

- Think of a problem or conflict that has arisen between the two of you in the past. As you proceed through the Self-Other Assessment, think of what each of you has contributed to that problem or conflict. Now imagine a space halfway between you at the 50 percent line. Take turns assessing and discussing your own part, good and bad, in that issue. Listen to each other. This exercise is directed at jointly creating a hospitable space in which your feelings can be spoken exactly as they are without fearing contradiction, lashing out, or rejection.

- The Self-Other Assessment is an opportunity to identify what's happening between you and your partner by listening without judgment and keeping the focus on yourself. Feelings of safety are allowed to develop by not interrupting or commenting and by consciously refraining from sending signals indicating rejection of what your partner is sharing. This is based on the 40-20-40 Model, which is a method for communication in which partners agree to contribute no more than 60 percent and no less than 40 percent of the caregiving in their relationship while reserving 20 percent in the middle for negotiation of giving and taking. What is this like?

Alternatives

- A difference between irrelationship and a partnership grown with compassionate empathy is that compassionate empathy energizes rather than depletes. Talk about particular relationships that left you feeling drained and frustrated. Discuss what you think was happening and *not* happening that made the relationship taxing. What would have changed that? What could both of you do to make that interaction more satisfying? Talk about how the work you did in the Self-Other Assessment, using the 40-20-40 Model, would be useful for opening up a space for give-and-take.

- Think of a relationship or an episode in a relationship in which you felt depleted and resentful. Discuss an interaction between you and your partner that left both of you with unresolved feelings. How could the Self-Other Assessment have changed how you treated this situation?

- What would happen if you made this alternative way of communicating a part of your everyday life?

Mutuality

- You've taken a major step out of the isolation of irrelationship into real relationship. While this experience is fresh, discuss how this looks and feels in this moment.

- Relationship sanity is the result of giving and taking in equal measure. Achieving and maintaining relationship sanity is done through the Self-Other Assessment. Now you see that the outcome of this is mutuality—a living, breathing, and growing space developed and maintained by all parties of any relationship. It's a space where, in direct contrast to irrelationship, empathy, intimacy, emotional risk, and emotional investment can develop and flourish as long as partners are willing to stay with it. Share with each other any incident or part of your life that comes to mind that could be changed because you were able together to walk away from your song-and-dance routine.

- Everything in your life together probably isn't going to be immediately transformed by your experience with this exercise. However, the exercise does put real tools in your hands—the DREAM Sequence and the Self-Other Assessment—that you can pick up when the old ways of thinking and relating pop up again. Talk about signals and cues that let you know you're being pulled back into your old routine and Performer and Audience roles. What agreements can you make with each other to short-circuit this when it happens?

- The purpose of this book has been to find ways to come out from hiding in dysfunctional relationships—irrelationship—and into intimacy—real relationship—together. The work you've done in the DREAM Sequence and using the Self-Other Assessment has taught you a way to open a space of intimacy and mutuality and keep it open. It is now yours. How does that feel?

Part Five

Encore

Cracked Open for Love

Chapter 13

Cracked Open at Last

If it hasn't already happened, one day soon you may be walking down the street or at dinner with friends when someone sneaks up under your radar and cracks you open. That's what happens when you let go of irrelationship, and you'll realize the depth of isolation you were living in without knowing it.

What does it mean to be cracked open? In James Cameron's movie, *The Abyss*, undersea explorers have developed a new technology—breathable liquid oxygen—that allows them to go deeper underwater than anyone has ever gone before. The problem was that the human body's instincts are programmed to keep liquid out of the lungs. If liquid does get in, every system in the body mobilizes to prevent death. In order for the explorers to tolerate the new technique that allows them to go deeper, they have to be cracked open—to learn a new relationship with their instincts and behaviors.

The DREAM Sequence does something like this for people brainlocked in irrelationship: it allows us to step out of old ways of thinking about ourselves so we can go deeper. Put another way, it helps us return to an older way of thinking about ourselves that allows us to rely on others.

But there is a flip side; you may have realized by now that doing the DREAM Sequence and practicing the Self-Other Assessment takes you in a direction you can't control and to a destination you can't predict. Accepting this type of vulnerability opens the way for the possibility of fulfillment and satisfaction long forgotten or never imagined.

Irrelationship Is—and Is Not—Like a Drug

Repeated use of a person, substance, or behavior that relieves deep anxiety is the core of addiction. In this way it resembles irrelationship, which, like addiction, can be managed but not cured. But irrelationship is also a set of behaviors learned early in life in connection with perceptions and interpretations of interpersonal caregiving. Potentially, then, the behaviors can be unlearned, or, in the language of cognitive behavioral therapy, "extinguished" and, at least in some cases, replaced with more effective relationship habits. Sometimes, however, the conditioning (neural associations) may be so profoundly ingrained in our thoughts and behaviors that only a workaround is possible, which leaves us vulnerable to falling back into old habits if the circumstances dictate the need for them. Going further, real relationships can be so profoundly unsettling that they scream for the reactivation of old defenses. Not surprisingly, temptation to resume our song-and-dance routines is strongest in our most intimate relationships.

If our song-and-dance routine is a true compulsion, then the high of relief shrinks with every hit. At some point, we realize the routine isn't working like it used to, and desperation starts. As in the case of the addict hitting bottom, this moment is ripe for the admission that we can't control everyone and everything around us.

Real relationships are full of experiences that can cause anxiety. Emotional health and well-being allow us to face anxiety rather than avoid it. As adults we can tolerate more anxiety than we could when we built our song-and-dance routines as children. Sometimes this comes as an epiphany not unlike the Bugs Bunny cartoon in which Daffy Duck is frantically building a fortress to keep Bugs out. In the middle of all this, someone asks Daffy what he's doing, and Daffy suddenly realizes Bugs is standing next to him casually munching on a carrot.

This process of compensating for anxiety finally distills into the irrelationship-based roles we play in our relationships. Even though these roles become ingrained and familiar, they're damaging because they limit a broad range of our perception of experience. Some of the experiences we deny ourselves are opportunities to challenge the self-imposed limitations to the roles we play.

Sticking to the DREAM Sequence makes accepting a new system shutdown a hard sell, particularly since brainlock has been cracked. Instead, the DREAM Sequence helps us drop the routine of trying to fix others and partner with them instead.

We Were Made for Love

Your Ignorance will be bigger than you
And it will kill you with a white death
With no noise
With no pain
And it will let you live
In your empty room
Not knowing what you could have been
—L.M.

In many ways, this poem (a graffiti on a restaurant wall) reveals the heart of irrelationship: cut off from oneself, and each other, we interact only in predetermined ways, producing a simulation of relationship that can withstand only superficial scrutiny. When irrelationship fails to deliver the security we're seeking, we slip undetected into crisis mode, gripped by conflict and fear. However, convinced of our own righteousness, we unwittingly recommit ourselves to the isolation that has haunted us all our lives. We exist in our empty room, neither fully alive nor fully dead.

True emotional, physical, spiritual, and intellectual engagement with another person gives reprieve from the pain of isolation. From this perspective, love itself is an interactional event. Through love, we can overcome isolation by becoming attuned with other people in a way that allows us a taste of what it is to be many and one simultaneously—to "contain multitudes."[1]

Once we start using our capacity for courage and the willingness to care about others and open our hearts to accept the same gift from them, we have begun to kick our compulsion to use the ineffective mechanisms of irrelationship to protect us from ourselves and each other.

Compassion and empathy beget connection and interconnection, leading to what we simultaneously hope for and dread: intimacy. Without empathy, what passes for love is only a patchwork of cultural confusion about feelings and relationships, delusions created by movies and television; our history of success or disappointment in romance; rumination on our failures; and all of this clouded by fear of being alone.

A major point of Erich Fromm's book, *The Art of Loving*, is that falling in love is easy—anyone can do it. But the scrapes, scruffs, and road rash can be terrible. Even so, harrowing as falling in love can be, walking through the day-to-day of *being* in love is even harder. Because modern humans are alienated from each other and from nature, we seek refuge from our aloneness in romantic love and marriage.[2] According to Fromm, real love is a rarity achieved only through developing one's total personality to the capacity of loving one's neighbor with "true humility, courage, faith and discipline," thus attaining the capacity to experience real love.[3]

The social-emotional interactions of people in relationships can expand each person's access to self-experience with powerful experiential and developmental consequences. In this sense, change becomes an interchange between the individual and his or her environment—remembering that, in this context, "environment" means "you and me," or our "each other." Irrelationship and our protective song-and-dance routines first developed in the environment of early childhood—namely, our primary caregiver. The techniques of the DREAM Sequence reconfigure that early, anxiety-ridden environment so we become for one another the environment of love and mutuality that we crave. We ourselves are the solution to our isolation.

Irrelationship's Greatest Irony

What is perhaps the greatest irony in irrelationship has been saved until now. In his appraisal of our culture's relationship with psychiatry and psychiatric medications, Charles Barber finds that changes to our brains' structure and function can be compared to similar changes brought about by drugs.[4]

Experience physically changes us. Learning itself is the modification of connections among neurons, fundamentally related to neural network activity. Similarly, profound empathetic experience—intimacy—is a robust treatment that can create change even at the biological level. Researchers studying the effect of empathy and compassion on the brain found empathy without compassion increased negative feelings, but empathy joined with compassion training increased positive emotions. Compassion appears to serve as a buffer against the potentially damaging effects of unchecked empathy, preventing burnout and empathic failure. Practicing compassionate empathy gives us a way to fearlessly bridge the gap between the story we tell ourselves and the real story told by those around us.[5] In real relationships, our true stories are validated and valued, and a new story is made possible at the intersection of you and me.

An Invitation
from the Authors

This book provides guidance to help you to answer the question, "How did I get trapped in and by irrelationship?" After Discovery, you are provided with simple but powerful techniques for getting out of irrelationship and finding the way to live in loving relationships.

Although life-long habits of mind and heart don't die from being called by their correct names, calling them out is a powerful signal to your anxiety and self-stifling habits that you're aware of their game and don't want to play anymore. That's a giant step toward embracing the spontaneity and unpredictability that make up real life.

Of course, you will go through periods in which you feel stuck. That's only to be expected as you learn new ways of living. Moreover, periods of seeming dryness are often needed preparation for the next burst of inward and outward growth, although this usually can be seen only in retrospect. However that may be, when you feel stuck, we encourage you to return to this book and your journal to regain perspective on where you've been and help you to think about where you want to go next.

We also encourage you, especially those who feel particularly isolated, to connect with our blog-based community of readers and others looking for a solution to stuck or stifling relationships.[1] Read our posts and interact with us and others who contribute. By all means, consider writing and posting your own experience of irrelationship, the DREAM Sequence, and recovery. No matter where you are in your journey, your experience can benefit others, and telling it will benefit you.

Notes

Introduction

1. Epigenetic changes are changes in the genome of the child caused by environmental factors affecting the parents that affect the way the gametes' (the sperm and the egg) DNA is read and translated into proteins.

2. Ainsworth, "The Development of Infant-Mother Attachment," 1–94; Bowlby, *Attachment and Loss.*

3. Bowlby, "The Nature of the Child's Tie to His Mother," 350–371.

4. Schwartz et al., "Altruistic Social Interest Behaviors Are Associated With Better Mental Health," 778–785.

Giving help is more strongly associated with positive mental health and resilience than is receiving help, making it easy to see how this set up ultimately comes to feel like a rip-off to the one who is being "helped."

Chapter 1

1. Searles, "The Patient as Therapist to His Analyst," 95–151.

The psychoanalyst Harold Searles believed that a child's first task in life is to provide a kind of therapy for his/her primary caregiver—usually the mother—and that the child's survival is subjectively experienced as being contingent on how well that job is done.

2. Clark et al., "Physiological Responses to Near-Miss Outcomes and Personal Control During Simulated Gambling," 123–137; Clark et al., "Gambling Near-Misses Enhance Motivation to Gamble and Recruit Win-Related Brain Circuitry," 481–490.

3. Inagaki et al., "Yearning for connection? Loneliness is associated with increased ventral striatum activity to close others," 1–24.

4. Žižek, *The Parallax View*.

Cultural theorist, Slavoj Žižek, presents an example of the difference between desire and drive. He describes a small child playing a game. The little girl is trying to grab a bright red ball. She wants the ball—capturing the ball is her goal. But her hands are small, and the ball is big. She repeatedly reaches for it, and it repeatedly slips away. But she wants that sense of mastery and competence. Besides, it's a bright red ball that she wants to hold in her hand. But at some point, despite the repeated frustration of her desire, her desire suddenly changes. She is having fun just chasing the ball. Her desire changes from wanting to win to wanting to prolong the fun of chasing the ball for as long as she can. This change in her desire, in fact, demands that she forget her original desire to catch the ball. This forgetting or ignoring the original desire, i.e. the loss of *self-possession*, is what drives the processes of obsession and repetition.

5. Sullivan, *The Interpersonal Theory of Psychiatry*.

Harry Stack Sullivan referred to states of dissociation as "Not-Me" states—versions of ourselves we don't know about and, moreover, *can't know about* because it is too difficult to imagine that we could be *that* person. Yet, we are (the "warts and all" versions of ourselves).

Chapter 2

1. This technique is referred to in boxing as *rope-a-dope*, a sneaky trick in which one party purposely puts himself into what seems like a losing position as a means of finally becoming the winner.

Chapter 3

1. Chansky, *Freeing Yourself from Anxiety: 4 Simple Steps to Overcome Worry and Create the Life You Want*.

2. Beauregard et al., "The Neural Basis of Unconditional Love," 93–98.

3. Graeber, *Debt: The First 5,000 Years*. Graeber discusses that debt is the perversion of a promise.

Chapter 4

1. Gallese et al., "Intentional Attunement: Mirror Neurons and the Neural Underpinnings of Interpersonal Relations," 131–176.

When a person activates his or her neural circuits by executing actions, expressing emotions, and experiencing sensations, the neural circuits are activated—

automatically by way of a mirror neuron system—also in the observer of those actions, emotions, and sensations. This shared activation suggests a "embodied simulation" that consists of the automatic, unconscious, and noninferential simulation in the observer. The researchers propose that the shared neural activation pattern and the accompanying embodied simulation establish a fundamental biological basis for understanding another person's mind.

2. Winnicott, *The Maturational Process and the Facilitating Environment.*

3. Ibid., 186.

4. Freud, *The Standard Edition of the Complete Psychology Works of Sigmund Freud, Vol. 14,* 243–258.

5. Bose, "Trauma, Depression, and Mourning," 399–407.

6. Schore and Schore. "Modern Attachment Theory: The Central Role of Affect Regulation in Development and Treatment," 9–20.

7. Eley et al., "The Intergenerational Transmission of Anxiety: A Children-of-Twins Study," 630–637.

8. Agazarian, *Systems-Centered Theory and Practice: The Contribution of Yvonne Agazarian;* Bion, *Experiences in Groups*; Redl, "Psychoanalysis and Group Therapy: A Developmental Point of View."

Fritz Redl introduced the term *role suction* in the United States to describe the power of a social group to allocate roles to its members. W.R. Bion's group dynamics further explored the ways in which the group (unconsciously) allocates particular functions to particular individuals in order to have its covert emotional needs met. Yvonne Agazarian has highlighted this process more recently.

Chapter 5

1. Goleman and Boyatzis, "Social Intelligence and the Biology of Leadership," 74–81.

Chapter 7

1. Klimecki et al., "Differential pattern of functional brain plasticity after compassion and empathy training," 873–879; Sette et al., "The Transmission of Attachment Across Generations: The State of Art and New Theoretical Perspectives," 315–326.

2. Goulston, *Just Listen: Discover the Secret to Getting Through to Absolutely Anyone.*

Chapter 8

1. Lerner, *The Belief in a Just World: A Fundamental Delusion*; Lerner and Simmons, "Observer's Reaction to the 'Innocent Victim': Compassion or Rejection?," 203–210.

The just-world hypothesis is the assumption that a person's actions are inherently inclined to bring morally fair and fitting consequences to that person—all honorable actions will be rewarded and all evil actions will be punished (Lerner and Simmons). In other words, the just-world hypothesis refers to the tendency to attribute consequences to—or expect consequences as the result of—a universal force that restores moral balance. This idea generally implies the existence of destiny, divine providence, cosmic justice, stability, or order and has the potential for cognitive distortion, especially when used to rationalize people's misfortune on the grounds that they "deserve" it (Lerner).

2. Alcoholics Anonymous, *Twelve Steps and Twelve Traditions*.

Chapter 9

1. Southwick and Charney, *Resilience: The Science of Mastering Life's Greatest Challenges*.

2. Borg, "Community Psychoanalysis: Developing a Model of Psychoanalytically-Informed Community Crisis Intervention," 1–66.

Although we use a type of group format that we call "Group Process Empowerment," we are indebted to the Chapter 9, Couples in Recovery Program for developing a group format—which, in combination with our usual format—has proved to be an effective means of helping couples access dissociated elements of their irrelationship song-and-dance routines, experience them at play with their partners, and work through the defensive dynamics that have, historically and unconsciously, made them seem essential.

Chapter 10

1. de Lavilléon et al., "Explicit Memory Creation During Sleep Demonstrates a Causal Role of Place Cells in Navigation."

2. Hofmann and Reinecke, *Cognitive Behavioral Therapy with Adults: A Guide to Empirically-Informed Assessment and Intervention*.

In cognitive-behavioral therapy, a strong evidence-based treatment for many conditions including obsessive-compulsive disorder, post-traumatic stress disorder, phobias, and other conditions, is a treatment known as *Exposure and Response Prevention*, which involves a structured approach to the process described

Chapter 10 Exposure to the distressing trigger facilitates "desensitization" of the negative behavior (for example, Performing) to the trigger (failing to "fix" the Audience, or the Audience's passivity) resulting in extinction, i.e., unlearning of the former conditioning. To the extent that old conditioning cannot be unlearned, practicing new behaviors and steps to avoid resuming old behaviors are also effective.

Chapter 12

1. Tronick, "Emotions and Emotional Communication in Infants," 112–119.

The safety provided by sensitive attunement between parent and infant facilitates the child's experience and expression of emotion, so he or she feels less of a need to rely on avoidant strategies. Part of safety is for the *child not to be left alone* in overwhelming states of negative emotion. If that happens, he or she will have much more trouble learning to manage difficult emotional states later in life, leading to difficulty in relationships. Instead of leaving the child alone, with adequate caregiving he or she begins to learn the technique of interactive repair.

Chapter 13

1. Whitman, "Song of Myself."

Walt Whitman emphasizes an all-powerful "I" which serves as narrator. In Section 7, the narrator has transcended the conventional boundaries of self: "I pass death with the dying and birth with the new-wash'd babe, / and am not contain'd between my hat and boots." Other passages suggest that the narrator should not to be taken as a single individual, especially in Section 51, "(I am large, I contain multitudes.)." Rather, he describes an almost universal, human experience.

2. Fromm, *The Art of Loving*, 79–81.

3. Ibid., vii.

4. Barber, *Comfortably Numb: How Psychiatry Is Medicating a Nation*, 191.

5. Klimecki et al., "Functional Neural Plasticity and Associated Changes in Positive Affect After Compassion Training," 1552–1561.

Empathy is essential for successful social connections, but excessive sharing of other people's negative emotions may be maladaptive and cause burnout. The researchers concluded that compassion training might reflect a new coping strategy to help a person overcome empathic distress and increase resilience.

An Invitation from the Authors

1. Look for our blog on the *Psychology Today* website at www.psychologytoday. com/blog/irrelationship. Your contributions will be read and welcomed.

Bibliography

Agazarian, Yvonne M. *Systems-Centered Theory and Practice: The Contribution of Yvonne Agazarian*. London: Karnac Books, 2011.

Ainsworth, Mary. "The Development of Infant-Mother Attachment." In *Review of Child Development Research: Child Development and Social Policy Volume 3*, edited by Bettye Cardwell and Henry N. Ricciuti, 1–94. Chicago: University of Chicago Press, 1973.

Alcoholics Anonymous. *Twelve Steps and Twelve Traditions*. New York: Alcoholics Anonymous World Services, Inc., 1952.

Barber, Charles. *Comfortably Numb: How Psychiatry Is Medicating a Nation*. New York: Vintage Books, 2009.

Belisle, Jordan and Mark R. Dixon. "Near Misses in Slot Machine Gambling Developed Through Generalization of Total Wins." *Journal of Gambling Studies* (May 2015): 1–18. doi: 10.1007/s10899-015-9554-x.

Beauregard, Mario, Jérôme Courtemanche, Vincent Paquette and Évelyne Landry St-Pierre. "The Neural Basis of Unconditional Love." *Psychiatry Research: Neuroimaging* 172, no. 2 (2009): 93–98.

Bion, W. R. *Experiences in Groups*. London: Tavistock, 1961.

Borg, Jr., Mark B. "Community Psychoanalysis: Developing a Model of Psychoanalytically-Informed Community Crisis Intervention." In *Community Psychology: New Directions*, edited by Niklas Lange and Marie Wagner, 1–66. Happague, NY: Nova Science Publishers, 2010.

Bose, Joerg. "Trauma, Depression, and Mourning." *Contemporary Psychoanalysis* 31, no. 3 (1995): 399–407.

Bowlby, John. "The Nature of the Child's Tie to His Mother." *International Journal of Psychoanalysis* 39 (1958): 350–371.

———. *Attachment and Loss Volume 1: Attachment.* New York: Basic Books, 1969.

Briere, John. "Treating adult survivors of severe childhood abuse and neglect: Further development of an integrative model." In *The APSAC Handbook on Child Maltreatment, Second Edition*, edited by J.E.B. Myers, L. Berliner, J. Briere, C.T. Hendrix, C. Jenny, and T.A. Reid, 175–203. Thousand Oaks: Sage Publications, 2002.

Chansky, Tamar E. *Freeing Yourself from Anxiety: 4 Simple Steps to Overcome Worry and Create the Life You Want.* Boston: Da Capo Press, 2012.

Clark, Luke, Ben Crooks, Robert Clarke, Michael R. F. Aitken and Barnaby D. Dunn. "Physiological Responses to Near-Miss Outcomes and Personal Control During Simulated Gambling." *Journal of Gambling Studies* 28, no. 1 (March 2012): 123–137. doi: 10.1007/s10899-011-9247-z.

Clark, Luke, Andrew J. Lawrence, Frances Astley-Jones and Nicola Gray. "Gambling Near-Misses Enhance Motivation to Gamble and Recruit Win-Related Brain Circuitry." *Neuron* 61, no. 3 (February 2009): 481–490. doi: 10.1016/j.neuron.2008.12.031.

de Lavilléon, Gaetan, Marie Masako Lacroix, Laure Rondi-Reig, and Karim Benchenane. "Explicit Memory Creation During Sleep Demonstrates a Causal Role of Place Cells in Navigation," *Nature Neuroscience* 18 (March 2015): 493–495. doi: 10.1038/nn.3970.

Eley, Thalia C., Tom A. McAdams, Fruhling V. Rijsdijk, Paul Lichtenstein, Jurgita Narusyte, David Reiss, Erica L. Spotts, Jody M. Ganiban and Jenae M. Neiderhiser. "The Intergenerational Transmission of Anxiety: A Children-of-Twins Study." *The American Journal of Psychiatry* 172, no. 7 (April 2015): 630–637. doi: 10.1176/appi.ajp.2015.14070818.

Freud, Sigmund. "Mourning and Melancholia." In *The Standard Edition of the Complete Psychology Works of Sigmund Freud, Vol. 14*, translated and edited by James Strachey, 243–258. London: The Hogarth Press, 1917.

Fromm, Erich. *The Art of Loving.* New York: Harper & Row, 1956.

Gallese, Vitorrio, Morris N. Eagle, and Paolo Migone. "Intentional Attunement: Mirror Neurons and the Neural Underpinnings of Interpersonal Relations." *Journal of the American Psychoanalytic Association* 55, no. 1 (2007): 131–176.

Goleman, Daniel and Richard Boyatzis. "Social Intelligence and the Biology of Leadership." *Harvard Business Review* 86, no. 9 (2008): 74–81.

Goulston, Mark. *Just Listen: Discover the Secret to Getting Through to Absolutely Anyone*. New York: AMACOM, 2009.

Graeber, David. *Debt: The First 5,000 Years*. New York: Melville House, 2012.

Hofmann, Stefan, and Mark Reinecke, eds. *Cognitive Behavioral Therapy with Adults: A Guide to Empirically-Informed Assessment and Intervention*. Cambridge: Cambridge University Press, 2010.

Inagaki, Tristen K., Keeley A. Muscatell, Mona Moieni, Janine M. Dutcher, Ivana Jevtic, Michael R. Irwin and Naomi I. Eisenberger. "Yearning for connection? Loneliness is associated with increased ventral striatum activity to close others." *Social Cognitive and Affective Neuroscience* (June 2015): 1–24. doi: 10.1093/scan/nsv076.

Klimecki, Olga M., Susanne Leilberg, Claus Lamm, and Tania Singer. "Functional Neural Plasticity and Associated Changes in Positive Affect After Compassion Training." *Cerebral Cortex* 23, no. 7 (2013): 1552–1561.

Klimecki, Olga M., Susanne Leiberg, Matthieu Richard and Tania Singer. "Differential pattern of functional brain plasticity after compassion and empathy training." *Social Cognitive and Affective Neuroscience* 9 (May 2014): 873–879.

Lerner, Melvin J. *The Belief in a Just World: A Fundamental Delusion*. Springer: New York, 1980.

Lerner, Melvin J. and Carolyn H. Simmons. "Observer's Reaction to the 'Innocent Victim': Compassion or Rejection?" *Journal of Personality and Social Psychology* 4, no. 2 (1966): 203–210.

Mascaro, Jennifer S., James K. Rilling, Lobsang Tenzin Negi and Charles L. Raison. "Compassion Meditation Enhances Empathic Accuracy and Related Neural Activity." *Social Cognitive and Affective Neuroscience* 8 (2013): 48–55.

Redl, Fritz. "Psychoanalysis and Group Therapy: A Developmental Point of View," *American Journal of Orthopsychiatry* 33 (January 1963): 135–147. doi: 10.1111/j.1939-0025.1963.tb00368.x.

Schore, Judith R. and Allan N. Schore. "Modern Attachment Theory: The Central Role of Affect Regulation in Development and Treatment." *Clinical Social Work Journal* 36, no. 1 (2008) 9–20.

Schwartz, Carolyn, Janice Bell Meisenhelder, Yunsheng Ma, and George Reed. "Altruistic Social Interest Behaviors Are Associated With Better Mental Health." *Psychosomatic Medicine* 65, (2003) 778–785.

Searles, Harold. "The Patient as Therapist to His Analyst." In *Tactics and Techniques in Psychoanalytic Therapy: Volume II Countertransference*, edited by Peter L. Giovacchini, 95–151. New York: Aronson, 1975.

Sette, Giovanna, Gabrielle Coppola and Rosalinda Cassibba. "The Transmission of Attachment Across Generations: The State of Art and New Theoretical Perspectives." *Scandinavian Journal of Psychology* 56, no. 3 (2015): 315–326.

Singer, Tania and Matthias Bolz, eds. *Compassion: Bridging Practice and Science.* Munich: Max Planck Society, 2013.

Southwick, Steven M. and Dennis S. Charney. *Resilience: The Science of Mastering Life's Greatest Challenges.* Cambridge: Cambridge University Press, 2012.

Sullivan, Harry Stack. *The Interpersonal Theory of Psychiatry.* New York: W.W. Norton, 1953.

Tronick, Edward Z. "Emotions and Emotional Communication in Infants." *American Psychologist* 44, no. 2 (1989) 112–119.

Whitman, Walt. "Song of Myself," *Leaves of Grass.* Philadelphia: David McKay, 1891–1892.

Winnicott, Donald W. *The Maturational Process and the Facilitating Environment.* New York: International Universities Press, 1965.

Žižek, Slavoj. *The Parallax View.* Cambridge: The MIT Press, 2006.

About the Authors

Mark B. Borg, Jr., PhD, has practiced in New York City as a licensed psychologist and psychoanalyst since 1998. He relocated to New York from Los Angeles after working for three years in South Central Los Angeles following the 1992 riots, developing theories and implementation strategies for community crisis intervention. This project received Congressional commendation and led to Dr. Borg's cofounding the Community Consulting Group, a firm that trains community stakeholders and other players in the use of psychoanalytical techniques for community rebuilding and revitalization. Dr. Borg's writings on community intervention, organizational consultation, and application of psychoanalytic theory to community crisis intervention have been published in various journals and collected work, and he has presented papers on his theories at academic conferences in the United States, Canada, Scotland, Ireland, Norway, Italy, Greece, Turkey, South Africa, Chile, and Israel.

Grant Hilary Brenner, MD, is a psychiatrist, psychoanalyst, and consultant in New York City. In private practice since 2002, he focuses on the treatment of adults facing serious difficulties in relationships, professional endeavors, and personal development, integrating multiple approaches to provide personalized care. Dr. Brenner takes a pragmatic and realistically optimistic position: People have the capacity to thrive and also have untapped strength and resilience. He teaches and supervises residents and therapists, is editor of the book *Creating Spiritual and Psychological Resilience—Integrating Care in Disaster Relief Work*, and is involved in not-for-profit work with Disaster Psychiatry Outreach as Vice President of the Board of Directors and as Co-Chair of the Disasters and the World Committee: Group for the Advancement of Psychiatry. He is an Assistant Clinical Professor of Psychiatry at Mount Sinai Beth Israel and Director of the Trauma Service at the William Alanson White Institute, in addition to other roles. For additional information, please visit GrantHBrennerMD.com

Daniel Berry, RN, MHA, has practiced as a Registered Nurse in New York City since 1987. Working in inpatient, home care, and community settings, his work has taken him into some of the most privileged households as well as some of its most marginalized public housing projects in Manhattan and the South Bronx. He is currently Assistant Director of Nursing for Risk Management at a public facility serving homeless and undocumented victims of street violence, addiction, and traumatic injuries. In 2015, he was invited to serve as a nurse consultant to a United Nations-certified NGO in Afghanistan promoting community development and addressing women's and children's health issues.

CPSIA information can be obtained
at www.ICGtesting.com
Printed in the USA
JSHW040845270921
19025JS00006B/8